KV-032-743

Danny Goodman

with
Katherine Murray

Fear WordPerfect No More

Danny Goodman

with

Katherine Murray

////Brady

New York   London   Toronto   Sydney   Tokyo   Singapore

Copyright © 1993 by Brady Publishing

All rights reserved, including the right of reproduction in whole or in part in any form.

Brady Publishing

A Division of Prentice Hall Computer Publishing
15 Columbus Circle
New York, NY 10023

ISBN: 1-56686-096-2
Library of Congress Catalog No.: 93-26095

Printing Code: The rightmost double-digit number is the year of the book's printing; the rightmost single-digit number is the number of the book's printing. For example, 93-1 shows that the first printing of the book occurred in 1993.

96 95 94 93   4 3 2 1

Manufactured in the United States of America

Limits of Liability and Disclaimer of Warranty: The author and publisher of this book have used their best efforts in preparing this book and the programs contained in it. These efforts include the development, research, and testing of the theories and programs to determine their effectiveness. The author and publisher make no warranty of any kind, expressed or implied, with regard to these programs or the documentation contained in this book. The author and publisher shall not be liable in any event for incidental or consequential damages in connection with, or arising out of, the furnishing, performance, or use of these programs.

Trademarks: Most computer and software brand names have trademarks or registered trademarks. The individual trademarks have not been listed here.

Dedication

To my daughter Kelly, who has an artist's eye, a quick wit, a loving soul, and a very proud mother.

Credits

Publisher
Michael Violano

Acquisitions Director
Jono Hardjowirogo

Managing Editor
Kelly D. Dobbs

Editorial Assistant
Lisa Rose

Marketing Director
Lonny Stein

Marketing Coordinator
Laura Cadorette

Illustrator
John Leonard Gieg

Book Designer
Michele Laseau
Kevin Spear

Cover Designer
Jay Corpus

Indexer
C. Small

Production Team
Diana Bigham, Katy Bodenmiller, Tim Cox, Meshell Dinn,
Mark Enochs, Howard Jones, Tom Loveman, Beth Rago, Carrie Roth,
Greg Simsic

Acknowledgments

Gremlin battling is an exhausting process. Special thanks to the exterminating efforts of the following people:

KiDDo Dobbs, Managing Editor at Brady, who is a truly amazing person capable of Great Things (a great secret weapon for any publisher lucky enough to have her) and one heck of a lot of fun.

Jono Hardjowirogo, Brady Acquisitions Manager, for giving me the opportunity to participate in another *Fear No More* project. I love these things.

Danny Goodman, series author, for his vision and thoughtful creation of this series. Also, on this title in particular, for his vote of confidence and support. Thanks for letting me help.

John Gieg, the Creature Guy, for creating the perfect little monsters that are tamed in the pages of this book, but who will, I hope, continue to live on. (Maybe a line of stuffed animals, John? Or T-shirts, Jono? Somebody call marketing...)

My agent, Claudette Moore, of Moore Literary Agency, for being so darned good at everything. She's the best advocate an author could have—much smarter than the Average Bear.

My kids, Kelly, Christopher, and baby Cameron, who are on summer vacation and have to put up with a mom who isn't.

My husband, Doug, who helps more than I could ever say and is the Best Daddy Ever.

About the Author

Writing computer books is a habit that Katherine Murray has learned to deal with. She was born in a small shack in Silicon Valley and left to be raised by a pair of PCs. Sure, they did the best they could, providing her with an 8088 education, but as technology increased, their mode of parenting became outdated. Today, Katherine is the author of 30 computer books and the mother of one desktop, one laptop, and one notebook computer.

Contents at a Glance

Contents

Introduction

Oh no. Not *WordPerfect.* Your friends have warned you about it. The people in the next office had to hire a trainer just to help the staff open the package. The people downstairs had to build a storage closet just to hold the documentation. You're supposed to learn this program and get *good* at it?

Who are they kidding?

We've all heard the WordPerfect horror stories. Well, take a deep breath and relax—most of them are not true. Yes, WordPerfect offers a gazillion features, but you learn them one at a time. In *Fear WordPerfect No More,* you'll take on those one-at-a-time tasks and master the little beasties. Just think of the satisfaction you'll have next time you run into a WordPerfect-phobic person at the Coke machine.

It *is* true that WordPerfect is one of the most feature-laden word processing programs of our time. It has everything from spelling checkers to grammar checkers to legal dictionaries to macros to tips for getting along with your mother-in-law. You may never need to venture out into the deepest WordPerfect waters; depending on the job you do, you may be able to just wade in up to your ankles. We'll even hold your hand while you do it (and swat at those little critters that come up out of the sand looking for unguarded toes.) Let's leave the drop-off for the people with the scuba equipment.

Confronting Your Fears

You may not want to admit it—most people don't—but your single biggest stumbling block is. . .really. . .*you.* Oh, you can blame WordPerfect for being so incredibly complicated or gripe about the number of features or the disk space it takes, but when it comes right down to it, learning a new program like this one is a scary experience. It's hard to believe that someday—perhaps months from now—you'll be sitting at your desk typing away like you've done it all your life (or, at least, for a month).

The biggest something that gets in your way is fear, and this type of fear comes in five flavors:

- Fear of messing up
- Fear of looking stoopid
- Fear of the unknown
- Fear of change
- Fear of fear

You know the fear of messing up: we've all felt it. Whether it's a Big One or a small one, those screw-ups scream "Amateur!" People peek over cubicle walls when they hear that embarrassing computer beep. Your officemates get tired of telling you how to add a footer time after time after time. When your boss sees you running frantically from your desk to the printer and back again, she rolls her eyes.

You know what they're thinking. Will you *never* learn? (That's what you're afraid of!)

That leads right into looking stupid, doesn't it? People are watching you, and you're floundering like a hooked bluegill. How in the world will you ever figure out how to set margins? You can't ask anyone—you don't want to admit that you don't know how. And what are fonts, anyway, besides those faceless things that chase you through your nightmares?

It's okay. Calm down.

Fear of the unknown is a big one. What if you never figure out how to set margins? What if all your reports are written in Courier when your cohorts are passing out printouts with all sorts of fancy type? What if you're still using the Glue Stick to paste on colorful graphs when other managers are including them printed right in their documents?

And then there's the fear of change. You'll recognize this one easily—it's characterized by those sudden intense pangs of loneliness for the old Smith-Corona typewriter. You find yourself rummaging through the supply closet, overcome with the urge to find the thing and hug it. Oh, life seemed so much simpler then. You typed a letter, signed it, folded it, and put it in the envelope. There. It's done. So what if you had to do the same thing—same letter, same signature—day after day after day? At least it was easy and you understood what was expected of you.

The last one—the fear of fear—is the little gremlin that paints a picture in your brain of you, six months from now, still as panicked as you are today. You haven't learned anything. Your computer still beeps. Margins still elude you. And everything you print—from memos to annual reports—are printed in that nightmarish Courier.

Take a deep breath and relax. Then invite all those little fear monsters to come on out and have a cup of coffee. Through the course of this book, you'll learn that those little devils that seem so scary right this minute are no more than figments of your imagination.

What You'll Find in Fear WordPerfect No More

In this book, you'll find a unique approach to dealing with your WordPerfect intimidation. The best weapon against fear in any form is education, and we've packed all the basics between the covers of this book. Specifically, you'll find that the following elements come together to make learning WordPerfect nonthreatening and (dare we say it?) perhaps even fun:

- A set of encounters, each helping you learn a new WordPerfect skill and dispel a demon or two

- A goal statement clearly defining what you'll accomplish in each session

- A What-You-Will-Need section that tells you, up front, the elements you need for a successful encounter

- Terms of Enfearment, which highlight the WordPerfect buzzwords you'll master

- The briefing, in which the main explanation of the encounter takes place, showing Things As They Should Be

- They're Out To Get Us, a section detailing what might happen when Things *Aren't* As They Should Be

- Demon-strations, which allow you to practice hands-on examples of the encounter topic

- Summary, which gives you a broad-brush overview of the topics introduced in the encounter

- Exorcises, a set of fill-in-the-blank, matching, multiple-choice, and true/false questions that allow you to test what you've learned and make sure that you've rid yourself of that particular encounter's gremlin.

Throughout the book, you'll see screen shots when you need them, and illustrations of those buggy little monsters pop up all over the place. Tables are also used, as needed, to highlight information. Additionally, you'll find numbered steps and bulleted lists in passages where extra emphasis is given to steps in a tutorial section or to items in a series.

What You Won't Find in Fear WordPerfect No More

The best books don't try to be all things to all people. You won't find a bunch of things in this book:

- No super-technical explanations

- No programming code (ugh)

- No esoteric references to procedures you'll never use in a million years

- No brain-melting macros

- No tricks that require you to drink a glass of water upside-down (which, by the way, is the only *real* cure for hiccups)

- No tacky references to other Brady books you can buy for more in-depth coverage of WordPerfect (although if you *really* want to know— *Perfect WordPerfect Documents* by Marianne Carroll is available)

In a bold attempt to give you only what you need to slay your WordPerfect dragons and get on the road to word processing wizardry, *Fear WordPerfect No More* helps you learn the basics—just what you need to get going—and then gets out of your way. No unnecessary hand-holding, verbose descriptions, or long-winded explanations (Whew! I'm out of breath!)

Who's Afraid of a Little Program?

Well, if you've seen the WordPerfect documentation package, you already know that this is no *little* program. If you've seen the way it eats the storage space in your hard drive, you'd call it something other than small.

But, mass and memory considerations aside, why should you be scared of learning a new program? Because it's there. Because it's new. Because your job—or, at least, your ego—may depend on it. Most of us teeter on the brink of learning a new program until something or someone shoves us over the edge. We usually don't pick up a few disks and think "Hmmmm. I've got a few hours to spare. I think I'll learn this new program!" If we've got extra time, we do things we want to do, like laundry or leg waxing or skeet shooting. Not word processing. Not *WordPerfect*.

Specifically, you can use this book to squash your WordPerfect gremlins if you fall into one of the following categories (figuratively speaking):

- You are being forced to learn WordPerfect against your will.

- Your boss has told you that you can never go to lunch again until you master the basics of WordPerfect.

- You begrudgingly admit that having a word processing program and being able to publish your own materials would help your business.

- Your employees have already learned WordPerfect and are making fun of you because you can't even write a memo.

- The newest junior manager knows WordPerfect inside and out and creates eye-popping reports that get everyone's attention (and you want to hang on until retirement).

■ You just want to write a letter to your aunt, and WordPerfect is the only program on this blasted computer.

■ Your friend said "Buy WordPerfect" and you did. Why? You're still not sure...

Whether the tasks you'll take on with WordPerfect are simple or complex, whether the number of gremlins that plague you are few or many, *Fear WordPerfect No More* will help you take those first few shaky steps into the Wonderful World of Word Processing.

Now, if you're ready, think a Happy Thought, and let's go. . .

What Is WordPerfect and Why Do I Have To Use It?

Goal

To help you come to terms with the fact that yes, you *do* have to learn WordPerfect and that yes, you *can* do it in this lifetime.

What You Will Need

A morbid curiosity to see what's coming. (You probably watch out the window for approaching funnel clouds, too, don't you?)

Terms of Enfearment

word processing	ribbon
commands	Outline Bar
pull-down menus	scroll bars

Briefing

You know the sensation: your palms are sweating; your heart is hammering in your chest; the top of your head tingles like you're on the verge of passing out. You guessed it—WordPerfect panic. The only thing you can do to lasso those magnified fears is to shed a little light on them (they scatter like roaches at 3:00 a.m.). That's what this section is all about (dispelling fears—not roaches).

What WordPerfect Is

Even if you've just come in on the boat from some unelectricized, unpopulated, thoroughly unmodern island (sounds nice, doesn't it?), you can figure out from the name that WordPerfect is about words. Making words perfect? Well, *that* may be pushing it.

WordPerfect is an incredibly popular program that allows you to write memos, letters, reports, brochures, books, gum wrappers, and almost anything else you'd ever want to type on your average-Joe typewriter. Not only can you write with WordPerfect, you can arrange the words you write, putting them in columns, pushing them up against the right margin, left margin...you get the idea. You can also change the look of the type to create different effects—professional or artsy, serious or light, humorous or post-humorous.

What Will I Do with It?

That depends—what do you want to do with it? (No fair saying "Nothing.") WordPerfect makes it possible for you to do any number of tasks—simple or complex—that require wordsmithing. Here are a few examples:

- ■ Writing letters to send to clients
- ■ Pounding out a quick memo
- ■ Composing the documentation for a huge, over-budget, research project (aren't they all?)

- Creating and laying out a brochure to advertise your company
- Writing a computer book (Hey! There's an idea!)
- Designing, writing, and publishing a newsletter
- Writing, fine-tuning, and printing a corporate report

But I Hate To Write!

Oh, don't let Mrs. Moser, your seventh-grade English teacher, hear you say that. She'll have you practicing on the board—topic sentence, three supporting sentences, and concluding sentence—over and over again.

WordPerfect, however, loves people who hate to write. Think you're no good at putting words together? Let WordPerfect check your grammar for you. Can't think of a specific word? Use the Thesaurus. Can't spell werth a durn? There's a whopper of a spelling checker built into the writing tools, just waiting for your eager keypress.

You still may not enjoy the process (it's something like childbirth. And if you haven't experienced childbirth...oh, never mind), but at least WordPerfect can put expert tools at your fingertips so that your thoughts are presented in as polished a manner as possible.

Generational WordPerfect

WordPerfect, like many of today's popular programs, has been around through several incarnations. The current version is WordPerfect 6. The earliest versions of WordPerfect took some flak because of a hard-to-decipher screen; users just didn't know how to select commands (which you use to make things happen) or how to call up the menus (which are the little apartment buildings the commands live in).

Other miscellaneous things you don't need to know about WordPerfect 6's ancestors are that just a few generations back, WordPerfect didn't allow mice (no pets allowed) and one of the methods of selecting commands required that you push numbers—yes, numbers—to select commands. Talk about a brain-split.

Be glad that you've got the WordPerfect you've got. It's the bestest and the fastest, and it comes with a free set of ginsu knives.

It's Got That Look

The opening screen of WordPerfect doesn't tell you much, but take heart; you're seeing more than users of the earlier versions saw. Initially, all that appears on your screen is a menu bar and a status line (see fig. 1.1).

Figure 1.1
The opening WordPerfect screen.

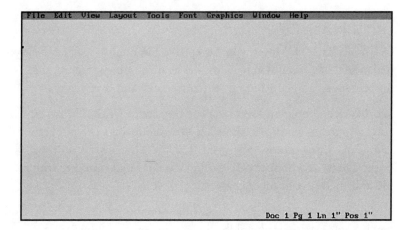

The menu bar is like a long row of apartment buildings, each housing a different menu with different commands. The commands in each menu have something to do with the menu name (which, hopefully, helps us locate what we want more easily). For example, the File menu includes the commands you'll use to work with files (see fig. 1.2). Logical, huh?

Figure 1.2
The File menu: Exposed!

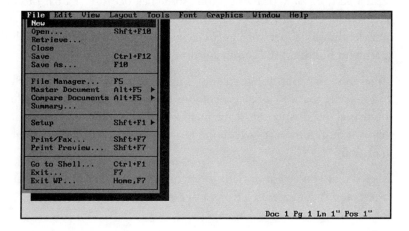

The status line gives you oh-so-important information about your file—so important, in fact, that you may never use it. If you're into things like knowing the exact cursor coordinates or caring what page you're on, the status line may help you feel At One With Your Application—the supreme state of computer consciousness. Otherwise, it's no big deal.

> When you first load up WordPerfect (which we'll get to in the next encounter—don't panic), what you're looking at is called text mode. WordPerfect also offers a graphics mode and a page mode, which displays the full page layout. You don't need either of these views yet, however, so forget I said anything.

Choice versus Overload

Some people whine that WordPerfect has too many features. This makes it hard for new users to find their way around and to get comfortable with the program. Some people go into a state of shock when they figure out enough about WordPerfect to open the menus but then aren't sure what to do with All Those Commands. Rumor has it that there have been several near-fatalities.

If you feel that WordPerfect lump rising in your throat when you begin looking through the menus, remember that the whole idea behind giving you that many different choices was that you'd be able to—someday, not today—find the method of using WordPerfect that suits you best. Right now, as you're learning, you'll try anything that works. (Oh, admit it—you know you will.) But later, when you've got some WordPerfect practice and are feeling a little cocky, you'll start experimenting with different key combinations, looking through menus you never use, or playing around with stuff that's Not Necessary (like drawing lines, making boxes, or using funky fonts).

Then, you'll be glad you've got this many choices.

WordPerfect lets you use either the mouse or the keyboard, whichever you're most comfortable with. Most users do both. They use the mouse for opening menus, choosing commands, and positioning the cursor. They use the keyboard for—uh—typing (I've yet to see a mouse that types as well as a human) and other things they can do more quickly by pressing a couple of keys.

Jargon alert: Key combination has become an accepted term for the action of pressing two or more keys together in order to carry out a certain procedure. For example, the key combination in WordPerfect for opening a file you've already saved appears in the File menu as Shft+F10, which means that you press and hold the Shift key while pressing F10.

Changing the Look

You don't have to leave the WordPerfect screen displayed the way it is. You can add other items, such as horizontal and vertical scroll bars (which help you move through the document—see the 4th Encounter), a type ribbon, an outline bar, and other items that probably make no sense to you now (see fig. 1.3).

Figure 1.3
There's no place like home, there's no place like home...

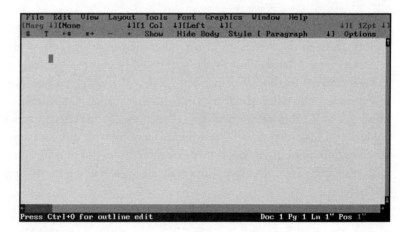

Felt your pulse go up a little, didn't you? Yes, the screen in figure 1.3 looks complicated. No, we don't expect you to know what all that nonsense means. Just for future reference, though, you might want to tuck away the knowledge that the top line beneath the menu bar is called the *ribbon* (it shows you important information about where you've set the margins, the selected style, the number of columns, the text alignment, and the font and size). Beneath that is the *Outline bar*, and along the right and bottom edges of the screen are *scroll bars*.

You can change the way your WordPerfect screen looks (when you know what you're doing) by using the commands in the View menu (see fig. 1.4). You can tell which features are turned "on" by the asterisks that appear beside the command (for example, there's an asterisk beside Outline Bar).

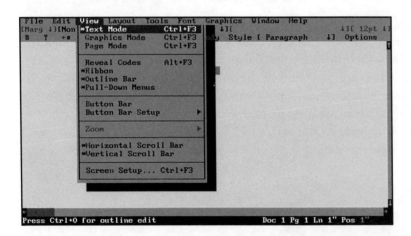

Figure 1.4
Changing the face of the WordPerfect screen.

You can change a bunch of the settings that control the way WordPerfect looks in one fell swoop (what, exactly, is a fell swoop?) by opening the View menu and choosing the Screen Setup command. A screen pops up, giving you the option of turning various things on and off. Experiment a little, when you're feeling bolder.

What WordPerfect Isn't

WordPerfect isn't the word processing program for everyone. You may not like the slew of features. You may not want mouse support. Pull-down menus may irritate you (must be a past-life thing).

You also may not have a choice.

If someone has put WordPerfect on your desk and said—perhaps not real politely—"learn this," you'll have to make the best of the situation.

WordPerfect isn't the panacea for all your business aches and pains. You can solve a lot of headaches—merge printing, newsletters, forms, letters, memos, reports, etc.—but you won't be able to automate your entire office with it. (But the folks at WordPerfect have probably come up with a sister product that can.)

WordPerfect also isn't easy on the checkbook. We're talking several hundred dollars here—not the $129 special that comes with a 35-word spell checker and has a little cartoon mouse on the front. Anything over that $200 cut-off point becomes more than a software program—it's a commitment. By signing that check, you promise to write, edit, and print, for richer and poorer, till upgrade do you part.

They're Out To Get Us

Oh, come on. What can go wrong when you're just starting out learning about WordPerfect?

Perhaps the worst thing that can happen is someone Important walking up and saying "Here's a new program. I need the annual report by Friday." Depending on how big the capital I in Important is, you may be in trouble. Learning WordPerfect is scary enough without also being under the gun.

If you're in this situation, try any of the following things:

1. Take a deep breath, let your eyes roll up in your head, and chant "Oommm."

2. Read through Encounters 2, 3, and 4 to learn the basics fast.

3. Look at the Important person and say "Oh, sorry—Friday is the day I shave my cat."

4. If you don't have enough time to try item #2, just do the Demon-Strations in Encounters 2, 3, and 4.

5. After you read Encounter 2 and figure out how to start WordPerfect, take the tutorial (in the Help menu) to get a quick, albeit boring, introduction to the program.

6. Pretend that you didn't hear him and start singing your favorite Aretha Franklin song at the top of your lungs.

Demon-Strations

Offensive WordPerfect

The best defense, as they say, is a good offense. So in order for you to get the jump on WordPerfect (before it jumps all over you), you need to think about the ways you can put the program to good use.

1. Start with a blank piece of paper.

2. Make three columns: **Task**, **By Hand**, and **WordPerfect**

3. In the Task column, write everything you do that involves words.

4. When your list is complete, read through each item. If it is something that you currently do by hand, put a check mark in the By Hand column. If it's something you could do with WordPerfect, put a star in the WordPerfect column.

Your list might look something like this:

Task	By Hand	WordPerfect
Write memo to Danny	√	★
Begin work on newsletter		★
Make grocery list	√	*Why?*

This list can help you identify the kinds of things you would like to do with WordPerfect, after you figure out which end is up.

Ready, Set, Go!

If you're working in an office environment and are learning about electronic word processing for the first time, you are used to doing everything manually: Insert the paper; turn the typewriter on; press Tab to move the typewriter ball to the correct place on the page for the greeting; and on and on and on.

But, you're so used to it that you probably don't even think about the millions of little tasks that comprise the bulk of your work day. Now is your chance to call attention to those little things that go overlooked (at least until review time).

1. Again, start with a blank page. (In just a few encounters, you'll be able to do this on the screen.)

2. Write down all the steps involved in doing your least favorite typing task. Be sure to catch everything (including White Out pauses and paper adjustment breaks).

1. Get the typewriter out of the closet.

2. Plug it in.

3. Get out the company stationary.

4. Find a piece of stationary that's not
   folded at the corner.

5. Insert the paper in the typewriter.

6. Take the paper out and reinsert it straight.

7. Press Tab as many times as necessary to
   move the typeball where you want it.

8. Type your letter.(Remember to press the Carriage
   Return at the end of each line.)

9. When finished, take the letter out and
   read it over.

10. Typos? Can you use correction fluid? If not,
    Start over.

3. Put your list away for future reference. Someday soon you'll see how much time and trouble WordPerfect can save you. We promise.

Summary

Discovering and facing what you're in for is half the battle in fear-conquering. This encounter introduced you—in broad terms—to the WordPerfect word processing program. You found out about a few of the ways

WordPerfect is used and learned a little about the overall program basics. The next encounter lights a flame under you by showing you how to start the program and begins with warm-ups for your own documents.

Exorcises

1. The current version of WordPerfect is Version _____.

2. Commands are stored in _____.

3. True or false: You must have a mouse in order to use WordPerfect.

4. You can change the way WordPerfect looks by _____.

    a. Changing screen color

    b. Running the setup program

    c. Using the Screen Setup command

    d. You can't.

5. Name three common uses of WordPerfect.

2nd Encounter

Time To Face the Music: Starting WordPerfect

Goal

To show you—oh, goody—how to start WordPerfect for the first time.

What You Will Need

Obviously, a computer. And WordPerfect (preferably already installed). And electrical power.

Terms of Enfearment

startup	cold boot
Windows	warm boot
DOS	installation
DOS Shell	directory

Briefing

We fondly call this tender moment—the contemplative silence just before power up—the Reflective Pause. This is the second in which you are surviving just fine, thank you very much, without the help of the electronic animal sitting on your desk. (Your computer, not the Garfield phone.) After you flip that power switch, you're going to hear whirring and clunking and then finally a hum that fades into the back of your consciousness and which you don't notice again until you turn the system off. Enjoy the silence while you can.

Turn That Puppy On!

It should come as no surprise that you can't run WordPerfect until you turn your computer on. If your computer is completely doornail-dead, you'll need to flip the power switch. In Electrode Land, we call this the *cold boot*, this rather violent jolt of electricity that shoots through the sleeping system. Poor thing.

The Coldest Boot

If this is the first time you've started your system—ever—check the following things before you flip the switch:

- ■ Make sure that the system is plugged in. You'll have at least one and perhaps as many as three power cords (one from the back of the system unit, one from the back of the monitor, and one from the printer).

- ■ Plug everything into a power surge protector, if you've got one handy. (If you don't, call down to the supply room and order one. Everyone needs protection from wandering surges. You don't know where they've been.)

- ■ Make sure that all the cables connecting the parts of your system are tight—plugged in all the way and otherwise attached tightly. You'll find cables all over—a mouse cable, a keyboard cable, a cable between the monitor and the system unit, between the printer and the system unit—just make sure that they are plugged in where they are supposed to go. (Of course, if they're not, you'll find out when you try to use them.)

■ Have your computer manuals handy, just in case...

■ Have your officemate standing by with a bucket of cold water...

When you've made sure that everything is ready to go, there's only one step involved in jolting that puppy into life: Find the power switch (it could be on the front, side, or back) and flip it to the On position.

> Not all computers come right out and say On/Off somewhere in the general proximity of the power switch. Some, instead, show a l and a 0 (zero means Off and l means On). One way or another, you'll figure it out.

Warming Boots

A warm boot happens when you restart a computer that was already started in the first place. When might you want to do this? After you install a program (not likely here, is it?); after your computer completely locks up and won't let you do anything else (*there's* a pleasant thought); or when your boss is walking by and you want to impress her by looking at your phone and saying "See, Garfield? This is called a *warm boot*."

> A friend tried warming (or, really, drying) her boots after a walk in the slushy Indiana snow by putting them in the oven at 300 degrees for a few minutes. Two hours later, the firemen didn't think it was very funny. Neither did her apartment neighbors, who had a heck of a time getting that odd rubber smell out of their curtains and carpet. Don't try this at home.
>
> The moral? Warm boot only when really necessary and be careful.

You can do a warm boot in two different ways:

- You can press the reset button on the front of your computer (it's that little button that says Reset).

- You can press the Ctrl, Alt, and Del keys all together and then release them. (Actually, you're supposed to press and hold Ctrl; then press and hold Alt; then press and hold Del (see fig. 2.1). The end result is that you're holding down all three keys and when you let them up, the computer says "Reboot!"—not audibly.)

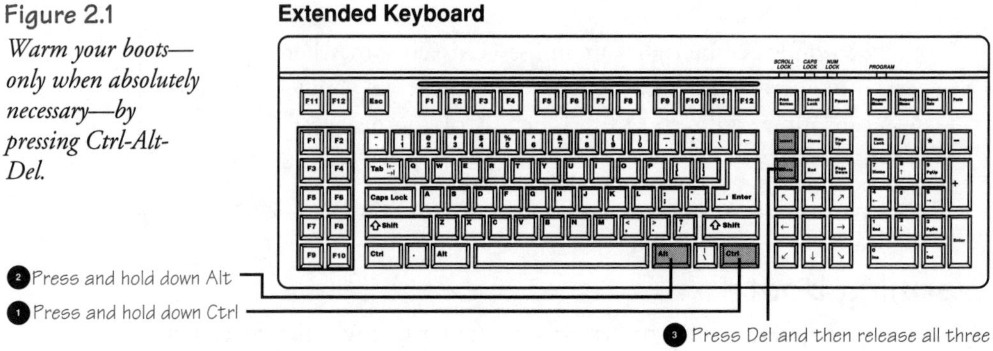

Figure 2.1
Warm your boots—only when absolutely necessary—by pressing Ctrl-Alt-Del.

Extended Keyboard

❷ Press and hold down Alt

❶ Press and hold down Ctrl

❸ Press Del and then release all three

Now What?

Okay, you've got the computer turned on. Some of what you see depends on who's been messing with your computer. And some of it has to do with how you use DOS.

DOS of the Damned. Never seen the word *DOS* before? Really? It's the secret code word that computer neophytes whisper to each other at a graveside initiation ceremony. It's also an acronym for Disk Operating System, the software that makes it possible for your computer to run.

What You Might See

Most of us see a pretty cold-looking DOS prompt with a little flashing underscore beside it. The prompt (another verb turned into a noun, thanks to the computer industry) probably looks like this:

```
C:\>
```

If someone has set up the computer for you—lucky you—you may be greeted with a special menu system. This menu (similar to the lunch kind) probably has some name or another at the top and lists a variety of programs, like Microsoft Windows, WordPerfect, Microsoft Excel, etc., depending on the programs already installed on your computer. If you see this type of menu, you're in luck. You can start WordPerfect by pressing the number or letter that precedes the program name in the menu. For example, if the line says

```
3.    WordPerfect
```

You can press 3 to start, or you can press the down-arrow key to move the highlight to that option and press Enter. (This may not be true of all menu systems.)

Even luckier still are those users who have benefactors who set up their computer to run WordPerfect automatically. It's possible, you know, to go straight into the program without even a single look at the DOS prompt. (Actually, it will appear for a second. Just don't look.)

But for now, we'll assume that you're on your own and are staring at that harsh, unfeeling DOS prompt. Before you can start WordPerfect, you've got to wander down the path to WordPerfect Land.

Getting into WordPerfect Territory

DOS isn't really as unfriendly as it looks. In fact, DOS has two personalities—the terse one that displays a single letter and taps its foot impatiently, waiting for you to enter something, and a much better personality (but still not anything worth doing cartwheels over), the DOS Shell.

The Shell is more popular with beginning users because you can actually see what you're doing. You can open menus, choose commands, and be comforted by having something to read on the screen. The DOS prompt, on the other hand, just sits there, waiting. You have to be able to pull the right command out of your hat at the right time, or you get beeped at and generally humiliated.

You can use the DOS prompt or the DOS Shell method to move to the place where your WordPerfect programs files are stored.

> *Jargon alert:* The computerese word for "the place where your files are stored" is *directory.* You store similar files in a directory and create many different directories on your hard disk. You might have, for example, one directory for WordPerfect, one for Excel, and one for PowerPoint. Within those directories, you would have more directories, which are called *subdirectories.*

The Prompt Way. If you are using the prompt (which means that you're the type of person who, when you realize you have a splinter, grits your teeth and pulls it out *fast*), you can change to the WordPerfect directory by typing the following line and pressing Enter:

```
CD WP60
```

The prompt changes to C:\WP60>, telling you that you are now in the WordPerfect 6.0 directory.

> If you are using an earlier version of WordPerfect (Hey—don't feel bad. If it ain't broke, don't fix it), your directory and prompt may be different. WordPerfect 5.1, for example, was stored in the WP51 directory.

Collecting Shells. If you're a DOS Shell user (which means that you, when you get a splinter, get bandages, antiseptic, peroxide, and gauze before you have a friend try to pull it out with rubber-tipped tweezers), you get to the WordPerfect files by following these steps:

1. Start the DOS Shell by typing *DOSSHELL* and pressing Enter.

2. Use the mouse to move the highlight (wiggle the mouse around— you'll see it) to WP60 in the left half of the screen.

3. Click the mouse button. WP60 is selected (see fig. 2.2).

The directory you're looking at.   Click these when you want to see
                                     what's on a disk in drive A or B.

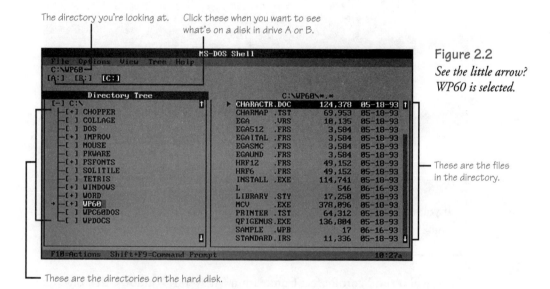

Figure 2.2
*See the little arrow?
WP60 is selected.*

These are the files
in the directory.

These are the directories on the hard disk.

Ways of Waking Up WordPerfect

Depending on the way you got into WordPerfect territory, you're now ready to use one of two methods to start the program:

■ If you used the DOS prompt, type *WP* and press Enter.

■ If you used the Shell, use the mouse to click on the down arrow in the scroll bar at the far right side of the screen. The files will scroll up, revealing more files at the bottom. When WP.EXE is highlighted, stop scrolling (see fig. 2.3). WP.EXE is the file that runs WordPerfect.

When it is highlighted, press Enter or double-click the mouse button. (Except that we haven't taught you how to double-click yet. See Encounter 3 for more information.)

Figure 2.3

Highlighting the big kahuna program file.

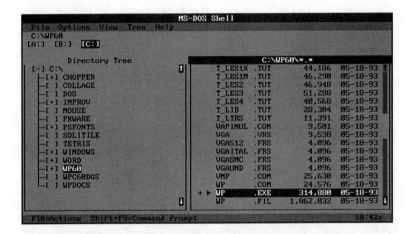

```
                              MS-DOS Shell
 File  Options  View  Tree  Help
 C:\WP60
[A:]  [B:]  [C:]

      Directory Tree                        C:\WP60\*.*
  [-] C:\                    ↑    T_LES1K  .TUT     44,186  05-18-93 ↑
    ├─[+] CHOPPER                 T_LES1M  .TUT     46,290  05-18-93
    ├─[ ] COLLAGE                 T_LES2   .TUT     46,948  05-18-93
    ├─[ ] DOS                     T_LES3   .TUT     51,288  05-18-93
    ├─[+] IMPROV                  T_LES4   .TUT     40,568  05-18-93
    ├─[ ] MOUSE                   T_LIB    .TUT     28,304  05-18-93
    ├─[ ] PKWARE                  T_LTRS   .TUT     11,391  05-18-93
    ├─[+] PSFONTS                 VAPINUL  .COM      9,581  05-18-93
    ├─[ ] SOLITILE                VGA      .URS      9,538  05-18-93
    ├─[ ] TETRIS                  VGA512   .FRS      4,096  05-18-93
    ├─[+] WINDOWS                 VGAITAL  .FRS      4,096  05-18-93
    ├─[+] WORD                    VGASMC   .FRS      4,096  05-18-93
    ├─[+] WP60                    VGAUND   .FRS      4,096  05-18-93
    ├─[ ] WPC60DOS                VMP      .COM     25,630  05-18-93
    └─[ ] WPDOCS                  WP       .COM     24,576  05-18-93
                              → ▶ WP       .EXE    314,880  05-18-93
                           ↓     WP       .FIL  1,862,032  05-18-93 ↓
 F10=Actions  Shift+F9=Command Prompt                        10:42a
```

If you're using the Shell, you can move through the list to WP.EXE quickly by pressing W and then pressing the down-arrow key once.

You can also run WordPerfect from within Microsoft Windows, that oh-so-phenomenally popular program that organizes everything in little windows on the screen. In order to set things up, however, you need to be at least a blue belt Windows user, so let's forget it for now.

What You'll See

Ta-Da! There it is—the WordPerfect screen. What style—what color (unless you're using a monochrome monitor). How much friendlier than the DOS prompt and more streamlined than the DOS Shell.

Okay. Enough bologna.

What in the world will you do with this screen? Where do you type? What are those words at the top? What language is that at the bottom? Figure 2.4 shows you what you'll be dealing with, and the next section explains how to decipher it.

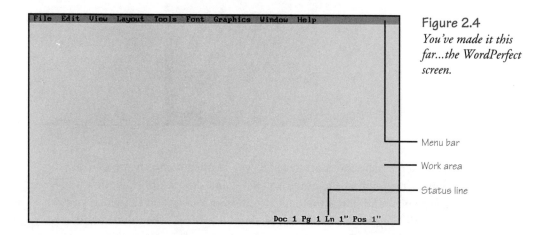

File Edit View Layout Tools Font Graphics Window Help

Doc 1 Pg 1 Ln 1" Pos 1"

Figure 2.4
You've made it this far...the WordPerfect screen.

Menu bar

Work area

Status line

What It Means

What you're looking at is WordPerfect's default display. You've got all the basics you need to get started writing purple prose. (Although initially, you'll see white characters on a blue background.)

Using the Menus

At the top of the screen, you see a line with nine words. These words are the names of menus, which house commands related to the menu topic. For example, commands that let you work with files are stored in the File menu. Commands that affect your view of the world are tucked neatly away in the View menu.

One letter in each of the words appears in a color different from the rest of the word. You can display the menu you want by pressing and holding the Alt key and then also pressing the highlighted character. For example, to open the Layout menu, you press Alt-L (see fig. 2.5). To open the Font menu, you press Alt-O. Get it?

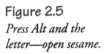
Figure 2.5
Press Alt and the
letter—open sesame.

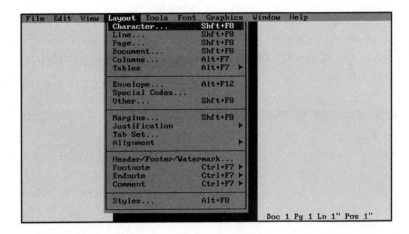

A quicker, easier, and more sensible way to open menus involves using the mouse. Just point at the menu you want and shoot...uh, click, that is. The menu opens and hangs there until you want to put it away (which you can do by clicking off the menu or pressing Esc). More about these hands-on kinds of things in Encounter 3.

Deciphering the Status Line

Initially, the only other thing that appears on the WordPerfect screen is the status line. At first glance, it's pretty hard to imagine what those chicken-scratchings mean. It could be calling you something rude.

Let's take it a piece at a time.

Doc 1 means Document 1. (Didn't know that you could have more than one document open at a time, did you?)

Pg 1 means—you guessed it—Page 1. Easy enough.

Ln 1" tells you the exact position of the cursor and its relation to the top edge of the page. In other words, the character you type at the cursor position is one inch down from the page edge.

Pos 1" explains the cursor's position in relation to the left side of the page.

As you type, the information in the status line is updated to reflect the cursor's current position. Seems a little like overkill, but you may be glad you have it someday. It's always there—just in case.

Why It Concerns You

Maybe it doesn't. Maybe you're ready to dive in and start batting words around on-screen. Well, be my guest.

But just think about what you've learned already. You know where WordPerfect lives, how to get there, and how to start the program. After the program starts, you know what the opening screen means and what it will tell you as you work. Pretty good for a beginner, huh?

Remember that what you see when you first start WordPerfect is the basic screen. You can also add scroll bars (which you may want) to help you move quickly through documents (except that the Page Up and Page Down keys work the same, if not better). Other items and displays are available, too. Experiment as your experience with WordPerfect grows and find the look that's best for you.

They're Out To Get Us

There aren't too many horrible things that can happen to you while you're finding and starting WordPerfect. But there are those straggly few.

Nothing Happens

This is a general, across-the-board, we're-in-trouble problem: the computer won't start. Well, you're not going to run WordPerfect if the blasted computer is broken. If you push the power button or flip the switch and nothing—absolutely nothing—happens, check to make sure that the computer is plugged in.

If the computer is plugged into a surge protector, make sure that the protector strip is plugged into the wall.

If it's plugged in and still nothing is happening, see whether the surge protector has its own On/Off switch. Is it turned on?

If it is and STILL nothing's happening, make sure that the power cord is plugged tight into both the protector strip and your machine.

It is? Okay, check the outlet. Plug in something else electric and see whether it works. If not, perhaps you've blown a fuse.

Oh. It works?

Hmmm. Time to call the technical support guy.

Wake Up, WordPerfect, *Please*?

Here's another one. You type WP, press Enter, and...nothing. Oh, go ahead, get up and do that I've-got-to-hit-something dance you do so well. Then, after a couple of deep breaths, answer the following questions:

1. Did you change to the WordPerfect directory? (Your DOS prompt should show `C:\WP60>`.)

2. Has WordPerfect been installed? (You can check by typing DIR and pressing Enter at the DOS prompt. If you don't see the WP60 directory, WordPerfect hasn't been put on your system yet.)

3. Who's bright idea was it to buy WordPerfect, anyway?

Demon-Strations

Movin' On Up

George and Weezie would be proud; you've learned to move though the directories of your hard disk without even knowing you did it. Remember?

1. When the computer is turned on and the DOS prompt is displayed, type the following line:

   CD WP60

2. Press Enter.

DOS changes to the WP60 directory (now displaying `C:\WP60>` as the prompt) so that you can easily start WordPerfect.

If you're using the DOS Shell, you do the same thing like this:

1. At the `C:\>` prompt, type *DOSSHELL.*

2. Press Enter. The DOS Shell appears.

3. Use the mouse to click on WP60, shown in the left side of the screen.

Now you're ready to start the program.

Pull the Rip Cord!

This is so easy it's almost silly to write it. Remember?

1. Type *WP.*

2. Press Enter.

If you got into this mess by using the DOS Shell, start WordPerfect like this:

1. Click on the down-arrow in the far right corner of the screen to scroll the files.

2. Highlight the file WP.EXE.

3. Press Enter.

In either case, WordPerfect starts, and you're ready to rock.

Summary

This encounter has been an important one for your WordPerfect foundation. You learned how to start your computer and get WordPerfect up and running. You also found out a little about the display that greets you once WordPerfect leaps into life. The next encounter takes you deeper into the mire by showing you how to use the keyboard and the mouse to get around in WordPerfect.

Exorcises

1. True or false: WordPerfect starts the same on all machines.

2. Explain the difference between cold and warm boots.

3. DOS has a split personality. Name the two ways in which you can use DOS and tell how they are different (in 30 words or less).

4. Explain two ways to open a WordPerfect menu.

5. Name that tune in four notes.

3rd Encounter

Typing 101 and Mouse Wrangling

Goal

To get accustomed to the keys you'll use most often and to exercise your mouse.

What You Will Need

Your computer turned on, with WordPerfect running; a keyboard; and a willing mouse (don't forget the little workout suit and the ankle weights).

Terms of Enfearment

QWERTY keys	cursor-movement keys
function keys	pointing
clicking	dragging

Briefing

Word processing would be pretty pointless if you didn't have a keyboard, wouldn't it? Those Pulitzer-Prize-winning thoughts rattling around in your head wouldn't be able to move from your gray matter to your computer's silicon chips without being able to force themselves out through your fingers.

The mouse, on the other hand, doesn't carry the same amount of necessity weight as the keyboard; with word processors, you can do lots of things without the mouse. A mouse is one of those what-would-I-do-without-it? items, like a dishwasher; before you have one, you don't particularly miss it, but after you get used to it, life *sans* mouse is unthinkable. This encounter explores both of these word processing tools.

Typing 101: Keyboard Fundamentals

You already know what a keyboard looks like. If you've ever used a typewriter, your fingers won't get lost on the computer keyboard.

Know Your Four Key Groups

QWERTY keys. Like a typewriter, the keyboard has all the standard alphabetic and numeric keys, in the same order (see fig. 3.1). These standard typewriter-like keys are known as QWERTY keys, named for the first six letters in the top left row (Why? Maybe because it sounds better than TYUIOP.).

It's a safe bet that you'll be using the regular QWERTY keys more often than you will anything else on your keyboard, just due to the sheer volume of letters in a typical document. Don't kid yourself, though—a certain amount of command selecting and option choosing will be involved. For most of those tasks, you can use either the keyboard or the mouse.

101-key Keyboard

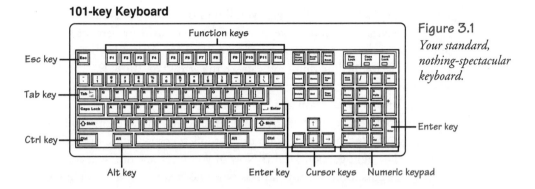

Figure 3.1

Your standard, nothing-spectacular keyboard.

Function keys. These keys are easy enough to find—they're the numbered keys that start with F on your keyboard (F1, F2, F3, etc.). Some keyboards have 10 function keys; some have 12; some have 15. As a general rule, function keys are over-rated; you may use two or three of them regularly, but you wouldn't miss them that much if they were gone. WordPerfect uses the function keys as part of key combinations, such as Shift+F1.

> Key combinations (the pressing of two or more keys at the same time) are one way WordPerfect lets you bypass opening menus and select commands with the mouse. Instead of opening the File menu and choosing the Save command to save your file, for example, you can press Ctrl+F12 without taking your fingers off the keyboard.

Cursor keys. Depending on the keyboard you're using, you may also have two separate groups of cursor keys. These are located between the QWERTY keys and the numeric keypad on the far right. The top group includes keys like Ins, Del, Home, End, PgUp, and PgDn. If you're like most people, the two keys used most in this group will be PgUp and PgDn. Home and End tend to do different things in different programs, so people don't take them too seriously. The bottom group of keys shows four arrows, pointing north, east, south, and west. As you might expect, you'll use these arrow keys to move the cursor in the direction necessary for your navigational task.

Numeric keypad. To the far right, you'll find the numeric keypad. On some older keyboards, the numeric keypad doubles as a cursor-movement keypad, and a separate set of directional keys is not provided. Newer keyboards include this double function (you can see the arrows on the 8, 6, 2, and 4 keys), but they also have the separate set of cursor keys. In order for the numeric keypad to function as a numeric keypad, the Num Lock light (in the upper right corner of the keyboard) must be on. Sound confusing? Try it: Press the Num Lock key (it's up in the top left corner of the numeric keypad.) The light goes out, right? Now, if you press one of the keys on the keypad, the cursor moves. If you press Num Lock again (and the light comes on), numbers appear if you press a key.

Specialty Special Keys

And there are those keys that don't fit into any category. They are nonetheless as important as any other key. These keys help you get places in the program, edit stuff, and select commands and options.

Enter. This key is the Do It! key on your keyboard. When you press Enter, you're telling the computer to accept whatever settings you've entered. Also, when you're typing text in your document, pressing Enter ends a paragraph and moves the cursor to the next line. Remember this key. You'll be spending quite a bit of typing time with it.

Backspace. The backspace key doesn't say backspace anywhere on it; it just shows a backward-pointing arrow. It's located in the top right corner of the QWERTY section of your keyboard. No matter what you're doing or what program you're using, the backspace key always does the same thing—moves the cursor one space back. Whether the backspace is a destructive backspace, meaning that it deletes the last character as it takes that step back, depends on the program and the settings you've chosen. When you first start up WordPerfect, the backspace is a destructive backspace, so when you type the word *Omigosh* and press the backspace key, as shown in figure 3.2, the h disappears. (And the cursor sits there blinking innocently: "Who, me? *I* didn't eat that h.")

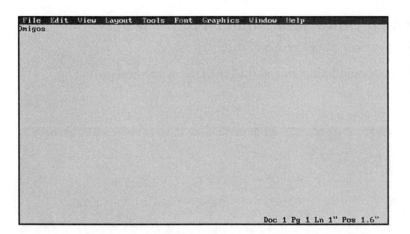

File Edit View Layout Tools Font Graphics Window Help
Omigos

Doc 1 Pg 1 Ln 1" Pos 1.6"

Figure 3.2
Demonstrating the destructive nature of the backspace key.

Tab. The Tab key is an unsung hero in a lot of programs, and WordPerfect is no exception. Think of how many times in a simple memo you press the Tab key. Does it complain about always getting the pinkie and never the index finger or the thumb, like more important keys? Of course not. And Tab saves you time and trouble, indenting your paragraphs, tables, and lists five spaces without you having to press the spacebar all those times. Dust off your Tab key once in a while, and let him know you appreciate him.

Shift. This is one of the always-been-around-so-I-hardly-notice-it keys. You had a Shift key on the old Smith Corona which you used to make capital letters out of smaller ones. Shift functions the same way on your computer keyboard, and now you have two of them. Shift is popular in WordPerfect as part of routine key combinations (for example, to open a file, you press Shift and F10).

Ctrl and Alt. These two keys are unique to the computer keyboard. In fact, there are two of each, so we're really talking about four keys. Ctrl and Alt are used as half of a key combination (such as Ctrl+F12 for Save). Ctrl is most often used to select commands; Alt, when pressed along with the highlighted letter in a menu name, opens the menu and also works overtime as a command-selecting key.

Anything But Those Timed Typing Tests!

Ready to put some of this keyboard theory to work?

That cursor should be blinking at the top of the screen as shown in figure 3.3.

Figure 3.3

Eyeing that sneaky little cursor.

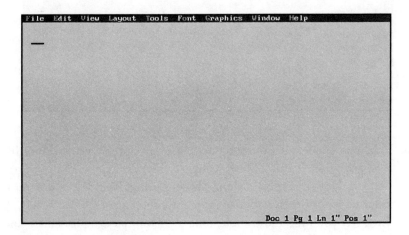

If your cursor is in a different place, you've pressed a few keys (like Enter) and you didn't even ask "Mother-May-I?" Your penalty is to use the arrow keys to move the cursor back to the top left corner of the screen. (Next time—wait for the rest of the class.)

Now cut loose and do a little typing. Go ahead and be creative: type anything you want. If your creative juices need a little jump-starting, you can practice using this paragraph:

> I've never seen a stripe-ed cow. I hope I never see one. But if I see a stripe-ed cow, I'd rather see than be one.

Anything unusual happen? Hopefully not. Your letters should have gone right through the computer and popped out on the screen as fast as you typed them. WordPerfect should have moved the cursor to the next line automatically as you approached the end of it—a bit of magic called *wordwrap* (the line break should appear right after the word *I*). Your screen should look like figure 3.4. (That's a lot of *shoulds* in one paragraph.)

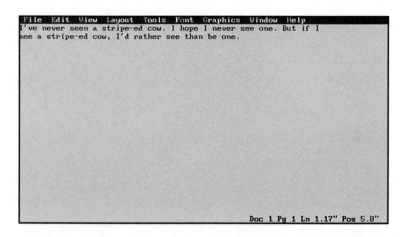

```
File  Edit  View  Layout  Tools  Font  Graphics  Window  Help
I've never seen a stripe-ed cow. I hope I never see one. But if I
see a stripe-ed cow, I'd rather see than be one.




















                                   Doc 1 Pg 1 Ln 1.17" Pos 5.8"
```

Figure 3.4
*Writing about cows
and udder nonsense.*

Didn't we tell you it would happen? The status line, in the bottom right corner of the screen, updated itself to show the cursor position. Another thing you don't have to worry about. Isn't WordPerfect wonderful?

Ready for the next step? Take a deep breath and press Enter. The cursor jumps to the next line.

Now press Enter again. The cursor moves yet another line down. (You just left the blank line between paragraphs.)

Another step: Press Tab. What happened? (The cursor should have moved in a ways.)

Now type this pearlish prose:

> The blue moose got loose from the city zoo. He wanted to smooch a
> puce goose, I guess.

Congratulations. You've taken the single biggest step in working with WordPerfect: you've written something. You are—really and truly—a WordPerfect user now. Look over figure 3.5; that's all the typing we'll do right now. Then go get yourself a cup of coffee and a Milky Way. You deserve it.

Figure 3.5
*Practice makes
perfect.*

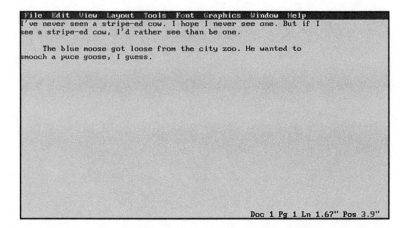

Yippee-Ty-Yi-Ho! A Mouse Rodeo
==

Well, this little varmint isn't going to get by with just hanging out on the
side of the keyboard while your fingers do all the work. Get out that lasso,
and let's get him moving.

> You may be expecting a mouse definition and a few technical terms
> telling you what the mouse does and what different kinds of mice are
> available. Sorry. We figure that if you're reading this section, you've
> already got a mouse, so you don't need to worry about selecting one.
> Suffice it to say that a mouse is a little hand-held thing you use to
> point to stuff on the screen. You click the buttons to say "Do It!" to
> the computer (like the Enter key, remember?) If you want to learn
> more about various mice nationalities, see *Fear Computers No More* also
> published by Brady (Oh, sorry—I said we weren't going to do that.)

Mouse Talk

When you deal with any animal (humans included), you have to know its
language before you can get it to do anything for you (just ask Doctor
Doolittle and the Giant Sea Snail). Here are a few important terms that
you'll need to know before you can consider yourself truly mouse savvy:

Pointing. This means to position the mouse pointer on the something you're thinking about selecting. When you use the mouse to point to something, you are moving the mouse body, and the mouse pointer on the screen moves right along with it. Move the mouse to the left; the pointer moves to the left. Move the mouse body up; the pointer moves up.

Clicking. This is the term used to describe a click of the mouse button. Which one? Any of the two (or three) buttons on the top of your mouse. (In WordPerfect, however, only the first button—the one on the left—is used to do anything significant. Some programs allow you to set the mouse buttons to perform specific actions, but that's too high-level mouse for us.) You click a mouse button when you want to say "Do It!"; for example, when you want to open a menu, you point to that menu and click the mouse button. The menu opens.

Double-clicking. An offshoot of the click is the double-click. A double-click is a quick two-click action; you click once and then click again, real fast. You use double-clicking to select files, options, and words.

Dragging. The action of dragging is a lot like getting out of bed on Monday morning: You stumble off to the shower with one foot dragging, like Quasimoto (Does that mean "sort of" moto?). When you drag the mouse, you press the mouse button and hold it down while moving the mouse's body. In WordPerfect, you'll use dragging to select a phrase, a line, or a section of text.

Mouse Events

Now let's put that mouse through some of its paces by trying out the mouse theory just explained. Get your rope handy, sit tall in the saddle, and wait for the green light: Three, two, one...go!

Pointing. Your mother told you that it's not polite to point. And yet, here we are, years later, practicing it. Put your hand on the mouse and move it upward toward the menu bar. The little block mouse pointer on the screen moves right along with you. Position the pointer on the word Graphics in the menu. You are now pointing to the Graphics menu name (see fig. 3.6). Notice that when you move the pointer over the menu name, the characters in the name change color. For example, when you position the pointer in the menu bar, it changes to black (on the white menu bar). When you move the pointer to the word Graphics, the characters appear while inside the black block.

Figure 3.6
Pointing for the sake of pointing.

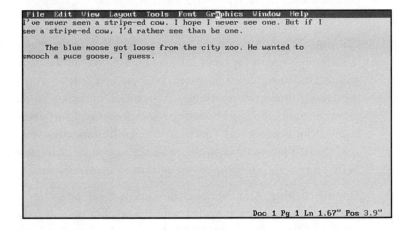

Clicking. This is about as simple as it gets. With your index finger (why do we call it that?), press and release the left mouse button. What happened? The Graphics menu (where you were pointing) opens (see fig. 3.7).

Figure 3.7
The result of a click? The open menu.

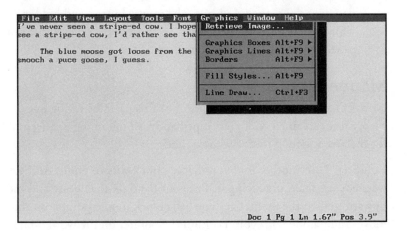

Wouldn't it be awful to open a menu and not know how to close it? Here's another click procedure: Just move the mouse off the menu—anywhere—and click again. The menu closes.

Double-clicking. First we've got to get to a place on-screen where a double-click will work. Move the mouse pointer—that is, point—to the word goose in the last line of text. Now double-click the left mouse button by pressing and releasing the mouse button twice, fast. As figure 3.8 shows you, several things happen when you do this correctly. First, the entire word (and the punctuation that follows it) is highlighted. Second, the phrase

`Block on`

appears in the lower left corner of the screen. Third, the value of position indicator in the status line (called `Pos`) is highlighted also. What does this mean to you? Nothing, yet.

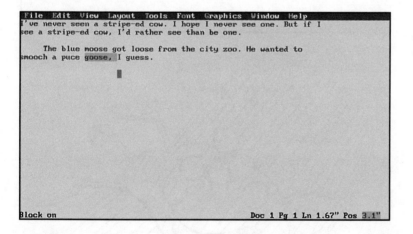

File Edit View Layout Tools Font Graphics Window Help
I've never seen a stripe-ed cow. I hope I never see one. But if I
see a stripe-ed cow, I'd rather see than be one.

    The blue moose got loose from the city zoo. He wanted to
smooch a puce goose, I guess.

Block on   Doc 1 Pg 1 Ln 1.67" Pos 3.1"

Figure 3.8
Double-clicking in action.

You can remove the highlighting on the word by clicking off the word anywhere (or by pressing Esc).

Dragging. Our final mouse event involves dragging. This mixes many of the tasks you learned here: pointing, clicking, and moving the mouse. First, move the mouse pointer to the *l* in the word *loose*. Then press and hold down the mouse button while moving your hand (and mouse) to the right. When you get to the space following the word *wanted*, release the mouse button. The phrase *loose from the city zoo. He wanted* is highlighted, as shown in figure 3.9.

Figure 3.9

*A little dragging goes
a long way.*

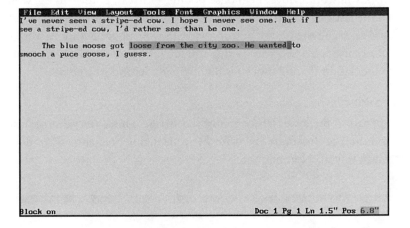

```
 File  Edit  View  Layout  Tools  Font  Graphics  Window  Help
I've never seen a stripe-ed cow. I hope I never see one. But if I
see a stripe-ed cow, I'd rather see than be one.

     The blue moose got loose from the city zoo. He wanted to
smooch a puce goose, I guess.




Block on                                    Doc 1 Pg 1 Ln 1.5" Pos 6.8"
```

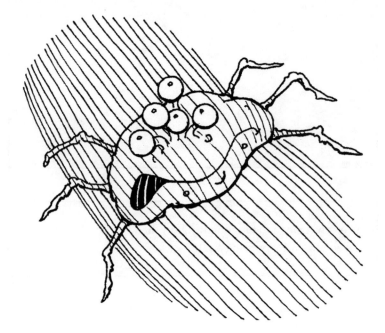

They're Out To Get Us

Luckily, there are not too many gremlins that can get into your keyboard or mouse. And even if—horror of horrors—something breaks, both the keyboard and the mouse are relatively inexpensive items.

Are You Sleeping?

You've been standing in line at the coffee machine, waiting for the hot water to trickle through brown and hot into the pyrex pot. It took forever. And as you stood there, waiting, you were agonizing about the huge pile of work you have to get through today. Composing memos in your head, you finally get your coffee and head back to your computer.

Okay, take a sip and sit down. There's the screen, gleaming blue with that flashing cursor, waiting for you to get to work. You think about the first memo you're going to write, start typing, and...

Nothing.

No beep. No characters. No nothing.

What's going on? If you haven't spilled your coffee on the keyboard (check your elbows—it does happen), you've probably got a keyboard that un-plugged itself. Make sure that the keyboard is plugged securely into the back of your computer.

Look on the keyboard and see whether any lights are on. If not, press Num Lock to see whether the light comes on. No? Your keyboard isn't getting any juice.

Try exiting WordPerfect and start again. (You'll have to use the mouse to exit instead of the keyboard.) After you exit to DOS, turn the blasted thing off, count to fourteen-and-a-half, and turn it back on. If the keyboard is broken, your computer will tell you so.

Maniacal Mouse

Every once in a while, you'll run into a strong-willed mouse with a mind of its own. You want it to go this way, and it rumbles and bumps and goes along—only begrudgingly. This, most probably, is a physical ailment and not a mouse attitude problem. Your mouse may have ball warts (which, as you can imagine, can make even the most pleasant mouse cranky).

Day in and day out, that little mouse scoots along the surface of your desk, and—admit it—your desk is not the cleanest place on the face of the earth. Dust and mucky substances accumulate there. Little pieces of M&M coating get dropped and remain there unnoticed. All kinds of sticky things can get pulled up into your mouse's delicate interior.

If your mouse is behaving erratically, turn him over. On the underside, you'll see a circle, inside which a portion of a ball shows. What may be happening is that gunk has adhered itself to that ball, making it move in a less-than-smooth fashion. You can open the mouse (don't forget the anesthetic) by moving the circle around the mouse ball in the direction it shows. You can then peer inside and clean the mouse ball with a little alcohol-dipped cotton swab. Be gentle.

Demon-Strations

Typing Trials

1. Move the cursor to the position following the last character of the text you typed.

2. Press Enter twice. The cursor moves down two lines.

3. Type the following:

   The zebra is a funny beast.

4. Press Enter.

5. Type the following lines, pressing Enter after each:

Who lives down where it's hot.
He's black and white straight up and down,
But spots he has not got.

Now this, combined with the text you entered earlier, should resemble the screen shown in figure 3.10.

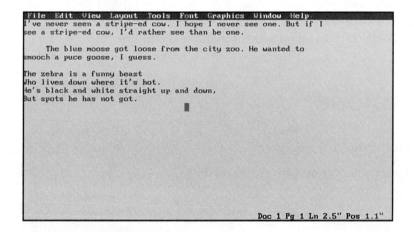

Figure 3.10
TFNAR: Typing for No Apparent Reason.

Mousercize

Ready? Okay! Everybody get your mouse and follow me:

1. Point to the word beast (*three, four*).

2. Click on the word beast (*three, four*).

3. Point to the word straight (*four, and*).

4. Double-click the word straight (*four, and*).

5. Point to the word black (*one, two*); press and hold the mouse button (*three, four*); and drag the mouse to the word up (*one, two*); release the mouse button.

Great! You did it! Everybody do some stretching to cool down and go get some orange juice.

Summary

You've learned some important basics in this encounter. Big milestones. Monumental word processing feats. Learning the basic layout of the keyboard and experimenting with mouse procedures is an important part of feeling comfortable with WordPerfect. Right now, finding the right key and remembering the right mouse action may seem a little awkward, but soon you'll be doing all these things without thinking about them.

Exorcises

1. What are the four key groups?

2. Explain what cursor-movement keys do.

3. What is word wrap?

   a. A cool street poem.

   b. Plastic covering that keeps your words fresh.

   c. An automatic feature that moves text to the next line when the current line is full.

4. What does pressing Enter say to the computer?

5. Name four mouse actions.

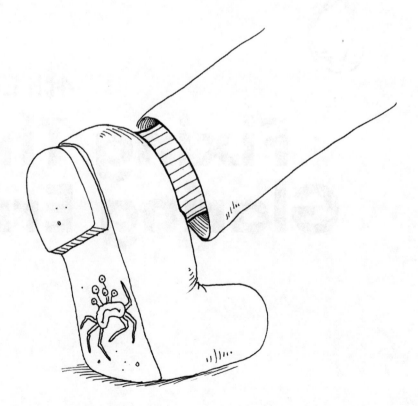

4th Encounter

Fixing Those Glaring Errors

Goal

To show you how to hop through the text patch and weed out those thorny errors.

What You Will Need

WordPerfect up and running and either the sample file we worked on last encounter or a paragraph or two of your own.

Terms of Enfearment

arrow keys	PgUp
PgDn	Home
End	scroll bars
Go to	Backspace
Insert mode	Typeover mode

Briefing

The last encounter showed you around the keyboard and introduced you to the mouse. This encounter gets out a magnifying glass and takes a closer look at the simple procedures you use to get to a mistake and fix it.

Getting There Is Half the Fun

After you've learned how to enter text and then find your way through the text you've entered, you've mastered a good part of any word processing program. You've already got the words in there; now you just have to process them. WordPerfect gives you several different ways to get to the places in your document you want to reach. The method you choose, of course, depends at least in part on your document (how long is it?).

Trying to make some sense out of all this, we've lumped "moving" into the following categories:

A *small move* is when you want to move the cursor a short distance: up a few lines, over a few characters, down a couple of paragraphs.

A *medium move* is when you need to scroll through some of the text on-screen in order to find the text you need. You might have to move a screenful or two either up or down.

A *big move* is a page-to-page move. You remember a phrase you used on page 10 that you wish you hadn't; you're working on page 1 now. You need to do some serious moving in order to get to that error.

Small Moves: Words, Lines, and Paragraphs

You learned a little bit about small moves when you were working with the mouse in Encounter 3. We deferred the cursor-movement key discussion, however, to this point. (Don't worry, we'll review mouse actions here, too.)

Keyboard techniques. When you want to move the cursor a short distance, you have four basic options:

| ↑ | up-arrow |
| ↓ | down-arrow |

| → | right-arrow |
| ← | left-arrow |

Each of these cursor-movement keys (also called *arrow keys*) moves the cursor one space in the desired direction. Want an example? Start with the screen in figure 4.1 (the cursor is positioned right in the center, at the beginning of the word *from*).

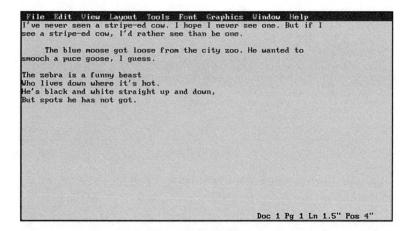

Figure 4.1
Getting ready for a little trip.

Now, if you press →, the cursor moves one character to the right, resting on the r in *from*. Press ↑, and the cursor moves one line up (and goes to the left edge of the screen, because that's a blank line). Play around with the cursor-movement keys until you get the hang of it.

Mouse moving. If you're using the mouse, moving a short distance is even easier. Just point and click. Want to move somewhere else? Point and click. The cursor follows right along—your faithful friend.

Medium Moves: One Screenful at a Time

When you're working with a larger document (one that includes more text than can be shown on one page), you need some method of displaying the unseen text. Again, you can use the keyboard or the mouse to do this.

You'll have to take a leap of faith here in order to see medium movement illustrated. You remember the text entries we added earlier? In order to have enough text to play with, we've had to add some more (see fig. 4.2). If you want to try out PgUp and PgDn (not to mention the mouse exercises), you may want to stop now and type in some of your own purple prose.

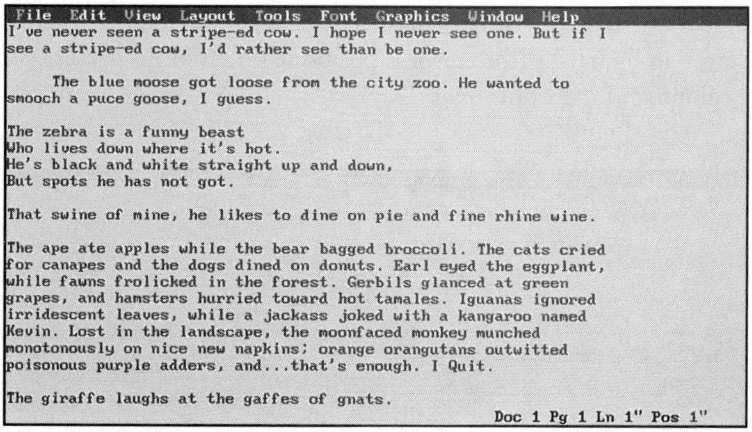

Figure 4.2
So, we added more text.

```
 File  Edit  View  Layout  Tools  Font  Graphics  Window  Help
I've never seen a stripe-ed cow. I hope I never see one. But if I
see a stripe-ed cow, I'd rather see than be one.

     The blue moose got loose from the city zoo. He wanted to
smooch a puce goose, I guess.

The zebra is a funny beast
Who lives down where it's hot.
He's black and white straight up and down,
But spots he has not got.

That swine of mine, he likes to dine on pie and fine rhine wine.

The ape ate apples while the bear bagged broccoli. The cats cried
for canapes and the dogs dined on donuts. Earl eyed the eggplant,
while fawns frolicked in the forest. Gerbils glanced at green
grapes, and hamsters hurried toward hot tamales. Iguanas ignored
irridescent leaves, while a jackass joked with a kangaroo named
Kevin. Lost in the landscape, the moonfaced monkey munched
monotonously on nice new napkins; orange orangutans outwitted
poisonous purple adders, and...that's enough. I Quit.

The giraffe laughs at the gaffes of gnats.

                                         Doc 1 Pg 1 Ln 1" Pos 1"
```

PgUp and PgDn—the keyboard movement keys. When you want to see text beyond the current display, press PgDn. WordPerfect scrolls the next page down. If you don't have more than one screenful of text and you press PgDn, WordPerfect just sits there and goes "huh?" When you press PgDn and you have enough text down there to see, WordPerfect displays the next screenful so fast you can't really see the change. Notice that the giraffe line is now almost at the top of the screen in figure 4.3.

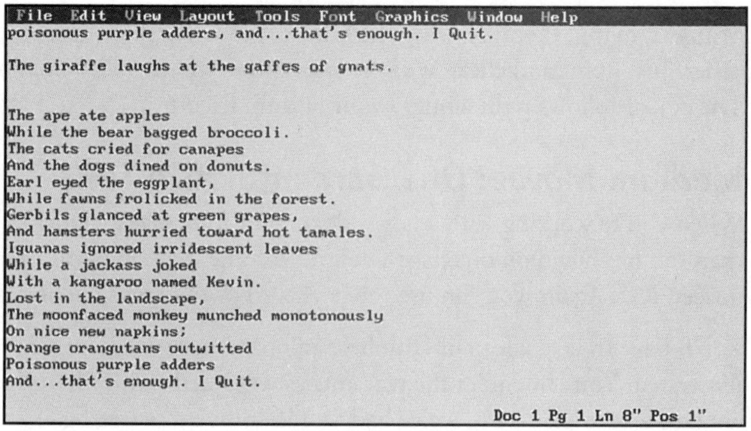

Figure 4.3
What's down there? Using PgDn.

```
 File  Edit  View  Layout  Tools  Font  Graphics  Window  Help
poisonous purple adders, and...that's enough. I Quit.

The giraffe laughs at the gaffes of gnats.

The ape ate apples
While the bear bagged broccoli.
The cats cried for canapes
And the dogs dined on donuts.
Earl eyed the eggplant,
While fawns frolicked in the forest.
Gerbils glanced at green grapes,
And hamsters hurried toward hot tamales.
Iguanas ignored irridescent leaves
While a jackass joked
With a kangaroo named Kevin.
Lost in the landscape,
The moonfaced monkey munched monotonously
On nice new napkins;
Orange orangutans outwitted
Poisonous purple adders
And...that's enough. I Quit.

                                         Doc 1 Pg 1 Ln 8" Pos 1"
```

Obviously, you can't use PgUp until you've moved down through a document. If you press PgUp when the cursor is already at the top of the document, WordPerfect will just sit there, wondering what you're trying to do. After you've used PgDn, use PgUp to move back up through the document.

> One other key you might use when you're finding your way through a text file is the End key. When you press End, WordPerfect moves the cursor to the end of the current line of text.

Middle-sized mouse moves. You may find that using the mouse is easier for almost everything when it comes to moving the cursor. Best advice for mouse cursor moving, however, is to turn on those scroll bars.

Oh. What's a scroll bar?

You can probably guess. A *scroll bar* is a bar along the edge of the screen you use for scrolling. And *scrolling* means to move text up or down so that you can see other parts of your document. WordPerfect gives you two different scroll bars: a vertical one (on the right side of the screen) that lets you go forward and backward through the document and a horizontal one (along the bottom of the screen) that allows you to move side to side.

To turn on the scroll bars, follow these steps:

1. Open the View menu by pointing to the menu name and clicking the mouse button. The View menu appears, as shown in figure 4.4.

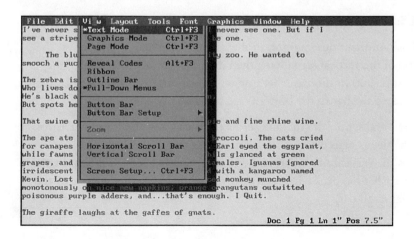

Figure 4.4

The View menu, exposed.

2. Move the pointer to Horizontal Scroll Bar and click. The menu closes, and the scroll bar appears along the bottom.

Now, if you want to add the vertical scroll bar, open the View menu again and choose Vertical Scroll Bar. Figure 4.5 shows the screen after both scroll bars have been added.

Figure 4.5

Scrolling through the text one day.

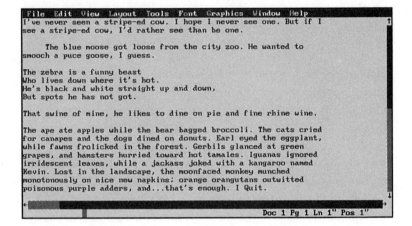

Using Scroll Bars. Earlier, you learned that to move from point to point within a displayed screenful of text, you just point and click. Working with scroll bars is a little more complex, but not much. You use the vertical scroll bar to move up and down through a document.

You can move down through the document in one of two ways:

- ■ Click on the down-arrow at the bottom of the vertical scroll bar.

- ■ Position the mouse pointer in the center of the long white bar (at the top of the vertical scroll bar); then drag the bar down to display the next screen. In this case, because we're working with a short document, we drag the bar to the bottom (see fig. 4.6).

The horizontal scroll bar (the one across the bottom of the screen), controls where the text is placed across the width of the page. This control is not as crucial as the vertical scroll bar, and you won't use it nearly as much. Figure 4.7 shows what happens when you drag the white bar to the left side of the horizontal scroll bar.

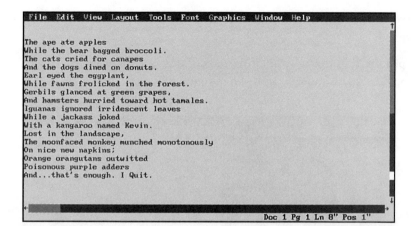

Figure 4.6
*Using the vertical
scroll bar to display
more text.*

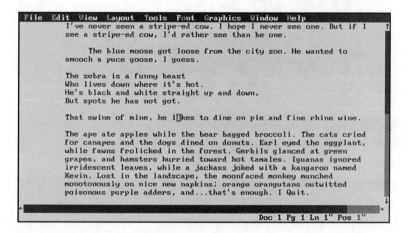

Figure 4.7
*The effects of the
horizontal scroll bar.*

Big Moves: Page to Page

The final movement—Beethoven's 9th—involves moving from page to
page. Initially, you might not think you'll use this technique often. Typing a
few lines of text seems like a big deal, not to mention *pages*. But think about
how many things you work with on a daily basis that will be multiple-page
documents: reports, newsletters, advertising literature, brochures, and on
and on.

When you need to move from page to page, you'll use the Edit menu's Go to command:

1. Open the Edit menu by pointing and clicking or by pressing Alt+E. The Edit menu appears, as shown in figure 4.8.

Figure 4.8
Going to Go to.

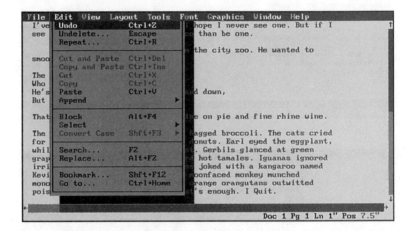

2. Select the Go to command by clicking on it or by pressing G. A small pop-up box appears, as shown in figure 4.9.

Figure 4.9
The itty bitty Go to box.

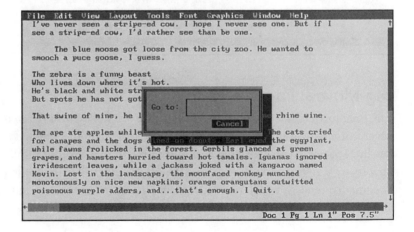

3. Type the number of the page you want to move to and press Enter. (If you want to cancel what you're doing, press Esc or click—you guessed it—the Cancel button.)

> You can use the Go to command without opening the Edit menu: just press and release the Ctrl and Home keys at the same time.

WordPerfect then moves to the page you entered. Along the way, it displays a small box that says `Repositioning`, just to let you know that it's going to considerable trouble to carry out your wishes.

What happens if you've only got two pages of text and you tell WordPerfect to go to page 73? WordPerfect tells you that it's repositioning and moves the cursor to the top of the file. Joke's on you.

> You can enter more than a simple page number in the Go to dialog box. You can move to the top of the page by pressing ⬆, the bottom of the page by pressing ⬇, to a specific character by typing the character, and to your previous cursor position by pressing Ctrl+Home.

Backspace, the Editor's Friend

WordPerfect has all kinds of cool editing features. You can spell check things, look for better words, and check your grammar. And we're not going to talk about any of those cool things here.

This section is about that regular-old-straight-head-screwdriver kind of editing tool. Oh, sure, you can have your turbo-charged motors and your lightning-fast macros, but you're still going to need Old Reliable.

The backspace key.

As simple to use as the eraser on the end of your pencil, the backspace key gives you the ability to wipe away characters like they were never there.

Misspell something while you're typing? Press that backspace key a couple of times and retype it. The mistake is gone, like it was never there. (If only all the mistakes we make were that easy to correct!)

But before you just climb in there and start backspacing all over the place, you need to know something about the dual—light and dark—personalities of backspace.

[Cue ominous music.]

Scoot Over—Insert Mode

When your first fire up WordPerfect, it's in a pretty forgiving mood. When you type and make a mistake, you press backspace, and—simple enough—the mistake is deleted. You can retype things correctly. This friendly mode is called *insert* mode, named because any text you type is inserted at the cursor position.

Let's try it. Move the cursor to the end of the line about the blue moose (third text line down). Click the beginning of the line and press End to move to the end of it (Confused yet?). Now, with the cursor positioned after the word *to*, press the spacebar and type the following:

> see Dr. Seuss

The characters after the cursor position move to the right to accommodate the text you added (see fig. 4.10). *Insert* mode. Get it?

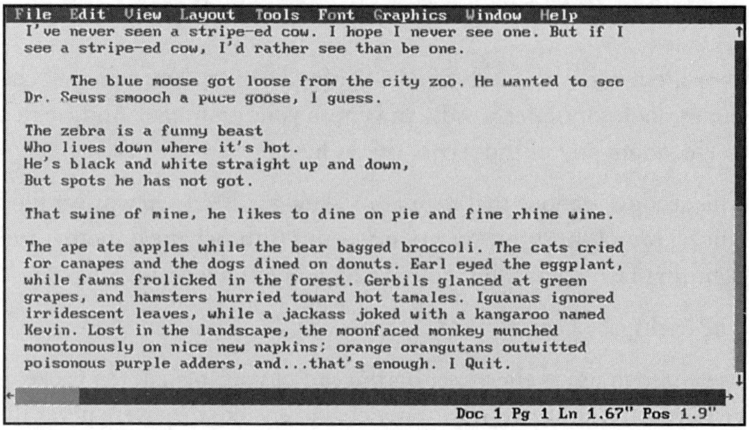

Figure 4.10
Come on in and join the fun: insert mode.

```
 File  Edit  View  Layout  Tools  Font  Graphics  Window  Help
 I've never seen a stripe-ed cow. I hope I never see one. But if I    ↑
 see a stripe-ed cow, I'd rather see than be one.

       The blue moose got loose from the city zoo. He wanted to see
 Dr. Seuss smooch a puce goose, I guess.

 The zebra is a funny beast
 Who lives down where it's hot.
 He's black and white straight up and down,
 But spots he has not got.

 That swine of mine, he likes to dine on pie and fine rhine wine.

 The ape ate apples while the bear bagged broccoli. The cats cried
 for canapes and the dogs dined on donuts. Earl eyed the eggplant,
 while fawns frolicked in the forest. Gerbils glanced at green
 grapes, and hamsters hurried toward hot tamales. Iguanas ignored
 irridescent leaves, while a jackass joked with a kangaroo named
 Kevin. Lost in the landscape, the moonfaced monkey munched
 monotonously on nice new napkins; orange orangutans outwitted
 poisonous purple adders, and...that's enough. I Quit.            ↓
 ←                                                               →
                               Doc 1 Pg 1 Ln 1.67" Pos 1.9"
```

When you're using the backspace key in insert mode, you get that gentle, one-character-at-a-time deletion. Just what you'd expect from a straightforward, logical program.

The Steamroller—Typeover Mode

But there's a darker side to our friend the Backspace key. Depending on the mode of the day and whether you're working with blocks, he gets testy and swipes away whole words at a time. And the characters we type aren't benevolently welcomed into the document but are used to kill off characters that were already there.

Why, oh why did anyone ever invent typeover mode?

Most of us have trouble with this concept only once. After that, after we've lost a paragraph, or a really good phrase we just can't remember, we learn our lesson. If you're working with valuable text, make sure that you work in insert mode.

Typeover mode is handy when you need to replace large portions of text and don't want to type it, then highlight the extra stuff, and delete that. Typeover lets you do it all in one stroke.

To turn on typeover mode, you press the Ins key. The Typeover message appears in the lower left corner of the screen, warning you that typeover mode is in effect.

When you're adding text in typeover mode, anything you add deletes the text that is already there. Remember how insert mode inserted characters in the text? Well, typeover mode runs right over those characters, replacing them with the ones you add. Want to see it?

If you're following along, the cursor should still be after *Dr. Seuss.* Press the ↑ key three times (or use the mouse) to move the cursor to the second line. Now, place the cursor on the apostrophe in *I'd.*

Ready? Press Ins. (Gasp!)

The Typeover message appears.

Now press the spacebar and type *hope his name is Fredrick.* What happened? The original line is completely gone, and this oddball phrase replaces it (see fig. 4.11). You can see how typeover can help you get things done quickly. But you also should be able to see how potentially dangerous it could be.

Figure 4.11

Using typeover mode to...uh...Fredrick?

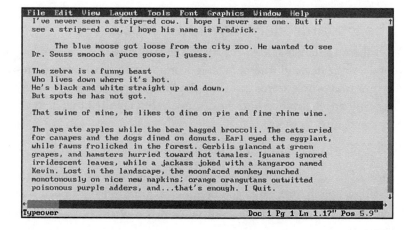

If you're using the backspace key in typeover mode, you delete the character, but the space remains. Be careful if you see the sign Block on beside the Typeover message, however, because if you press the backspace key now, all highlighted text will be deleted.

Save Me, Undo!

Luckily, WordPerfect offers a feature for those of us waiting for a caped crusader to come to our rescue. The Undo command, tucked neatly away inside the Edit menu, can return to us text we thought was lost forever.

What's the limit of Undo's capabilities? You can only Undo what you just did. So if you delete the word *kangaroo*, open the Edit menu, and choose Undo, the word is returned. Figure 4.12 shows you where the Undo command lives.

Okay, so we can save the last thing we blew away. But what if you delete *kangaroo* and then delete *orangutans*? You're stuck, right?

Maybe not.

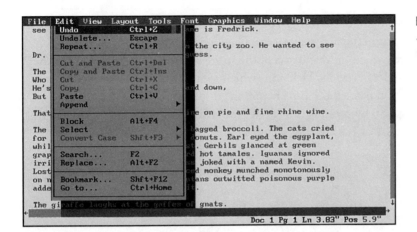

Figure 4.12
*Saving a kangaroo
with Undo.*

An extra bonus: Undelete. WordPerfect also has an Undelete command for
those of us who are always throwing away things we wish we had later.
Undelete can return to you the last three items you deleted; so stop and
think before deleting number four.

If you deleted *kangaroo* and then *orangutans* and decide you need *kangaroo*
after all, position the cursor where you wish the word was, open the Edit
menu and choose Undelete. (Or, if you really want to do it quick, just press
Esc.) The Undelete dialog box appears, as shown in figure 4.13.

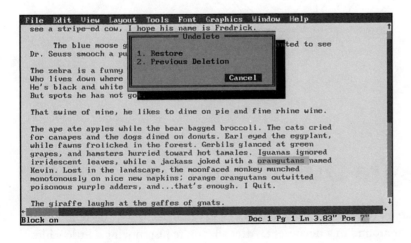

Figure 4.13
*Undeleting orangu-
tans and kangaroos.*

I know what you're thinking: You're supposed to see *kangaroo*, and this crazy program returned *orangutans*. The Undelete box gives you the option of Restore (which means to accept the word WordPerfect is plugging in the space) or select Previous Deletion (which means WordPerfect will look at the word you deleted the time before the displayed word). Choose the second option by pressing 2 or P. WordPerfect then displays *kangaroo* in the space. Press 1 or R to restore the text.

They're Out To Get Us

There aren't too many terrible mistakes you can make when you're moving the cursor around in a document. After all, you're just moving a little white underscore; you're not doing any damage to the text.

The danger comes in making corrections and confusing insert and typeover modes. You haven't learned to make any sweeping text changes (like marking blocks of text and copying them to other locations), but it is possible to start typing blindly (perhaps reading from something while you type) and overtype a slew of existing text.

Check that bottom left corner of your screen carefully before you begin typing to make sure that Insert mode—not typeover mode—is in effect. If the message Typeover appears in the lower left corner, press the Ins key to remove the message and return the program to insert mode.

Demon-Strations

Go Straight To Jail—Do Not Pass Go, Do Not Collect $200

There's always someone ready to tell us where to go, isn't there? The Go to command will help us get there.

1. Open the Edit menu.

2. Choose the Go to command. The Go to dialog box appears.

3. Type 1 to move to the top of the first page of the document. (Or, if you'd rather go somewhere else, type that document location.)

4. Press Enter. And Voila.

Dear Diary: It's 3:00 on Friday afternoon, and my boss left early. I was working on the quarterly report due Monday morning, when I was suddenly overtaken with an urge to go to the Bahamas. Without knowing what was controlling me, my hand reached for the mouse...I opened the Edit menu...selected the Go to command...and typed *Bahamas*. Here I am, listening to reggae and relaxing on the beach. Wish you were here.

Text Hide-and-Seek

Let's get that Fredrick thing out of there.

1. Use the mouse to move the cursor to the space following I in the second line of text.

2. Press Ins to turn on Typeover mode.

3. Type the following:

   You'd rather see than be one.

Your screen now looks like the one shown in figure 4.14.

Figure 4.14
What's an onek?

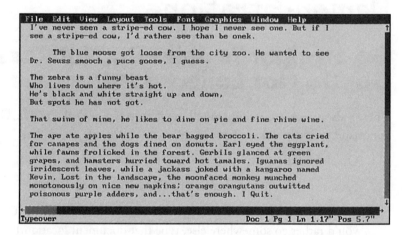

Hmmmm. Something's not right. We have an extra k at the end of the line. To fix it, follow these steps:

1. Press Ins to turn on insert mode.

2. Press Del. The extra k should be deleted.

Summary

This encounter explained some of the up-close-and-personal aspects to moving around within a document. You learned that there are different techniques to use depending on how far you want to move and how long your document is. Additionally, you found out about the backspace key and the profitable and precarious nature of insert and typeover modes. The next encounter introduces you to character makeovers using fonts, sizes, and styles.

Exorcises

1. Mix and match the right terms with the right items:

    _____ Words   a. Medium movement
    _____ Pages   b. Small movement
    _____ Lines   c. Big movement
    _____ Paragraphs
    _____ Characters
    _____ Screenfuls

2. What are scroll bars and why would you use them?

3. True or false: You can search for more than page numbers with Go to.

4. In insert mode, when you enter text _____

    a. The text overwrites existing letters

    b. It goes into a separate file that you can later insert into the document.

    c. The existing text moves over to make room for the new stuff.

5. In typeover mode, when you enter text _____

    a. The characters at the cursor position are replaced.

    b. The existing text moves over to make room for the new text.

    c. Nothing happens.

    d. Dominos delivers a pizza you didn't order.

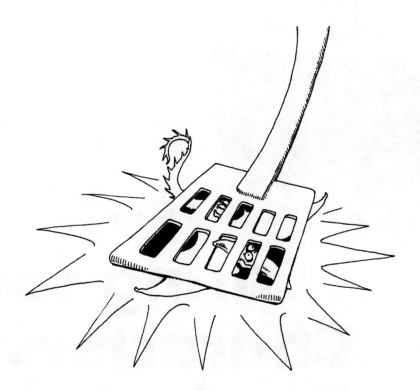

Caring for Characters: Tomfoolery about Fonts

Goal

To help you set the mood, with fonts.

What You Will Need

Same old stuff: WordPerfect up and running (sounds like a book title), a few lines of text (not necessarily what we've been working on for the last two encounters), and a willingness to follow instructions blindly to an unknown end.

Terms of Enfearment

fonts	fontanel
typeface	style
attribute	pinash

Briefing

Fonts are those things you think you need even when you're not sure what they are. It's a kind of watermark: "How many fonts do you have?" Researchers are trying to prove that the number of fonts you have is directly related to your IQ.

Do you need fonts to produce text on paper? No. Then why mess with them?

Once upon a time, we were limited only to typewriterish characters. Those blocky little ugly things had no spark, no life, no personality. We wrote our memos, reports, brochures, and handouts, knowing that our text was less than exciting. But what could we do?

Enter: Fonts. Style! Pinash! Excitement! A hundred and thirty-six flavors!

Now you can shout at your audience, whisper, coo lovingly (I'd like to see that), or coerce. You can make firm statements or lighthearted puns. You can find the look for your characters that matches the feel of your message.

Funny about Fonts

You may have heard that fonts are hard to deal with; that they cause headaches and high blood pressure; that they are better left to Those With Computer Experience.

Depending on the individual experience of the person you're talking to, you may hear Fantastic Font stories or Fonts From Hell. Don't put too much stock in other people's font experiences. You've got to get out there and have your own.

What Is a Font?

A *font* is a funny word that describes text in a certain typeface, style, and size.

Huh?

Okay, so we're defining jargon with jargon. Fonts come in different families, which are called *typefaces*. One popular typeface is Times Roman. Another is Helvetica. You'll find a trillion different typefaces coexisting in the publishing world.

> The word *typeface* is used in both computer and real-life typesetting. It means the same thing in both worlds. To your computer, a font is really a set of instructions that tells it to create a character in a certain way. Not all printers can print a variety of fonts (check your printer manual to be sure).

Each character has several characteristics, called *attributes*. It has a font family to belong to. It has a certain size, and it has a certain style. (Kind of like classifying children: This one belongs to the Murray family, is 42-inches tall, and is really LOUD.)

For example, one font might be

Times Roman	(that's the typeface)
10-point	(that's the size)
Bold	(that's the style)

When you apply the font to words, it looks like this:

This is an example of Times Roman 10-point bold text.

Why Do I Care?

Pretty testy question, isn't it? You may not care about fonts if you print only memos every third Tuesday. If you don't spend a lot of time with your word processing work and don't particularly care what it looks like, don't fool with fonts. They won't help you.

If you are on the chopping block every week, however, having to come up with attention-getting reports, cool training handouts, nice quarterly reports, and so on, fonts will be an important part of your word processing experience. Fonts really do make your words look—and sometimes sound—better.

When you care about the reaction of your readers, using fonts effectively can really add to the oomph of your publication.

What Kinds Are Out There?

This is a confusing question for most of us. Remember that fonts are really software instructions, like any programming code, that tell your computer how to make the characters you want. These instructions come in two varieties: screen fonts and printer fonts.

Screen fonts. Using screen fonts allows you to see more accurately what your document will look like when you print. If you're using Times Roman, for example, but the characters on your monitor are something else, your printed document will look much different from the on-screen version. To take care of this discrepancy, most word processing programs—and WordPerfect is no exception—offer a preview mode.

> *Jargon alert:* You'll see the term WYSIWYG used to describe this on-screen-and-in-print feature. WYSIWYG is an acronym for "what-you-see-is-what-you-get." Cute, huh? Somewhere there's a program developer that's really proud of that.

Printer fonts. These are the important ones. If your printer can't handle fonts (and not all printers can), you're not going to get your text to look much different. No way, no how. All printers can change the way the font looks a little bit, even the lowest of the low. For example, for rough draft and editing work, I use my trusty old Panasonic dot-matrix printer. Sure, the thing can print different fonts—a bunch of them. Dozens of flavors of Courier (see fig. 5.1). How exciting.

For final drafts and publishing projects, I use a more well-endowed printer, one with Postscript capability. The QMS is capable of printing 36 different fonts in a variety of type families (see fig. 5.2). And it has it's own memory, so I can use other fonts (remember, a font is really a set of computer instructions) by having the program send the description to the printer at print time.

```
This is Courier 10-point normal.

This is Courier 10-point bold.

This is Courier 10-point italic.

This is (*yawn*) Courier 12-point normal.

This is Courier 12-point bold.

This is (*snore*) Courier 12-point
italic.

This is Courier z...z...z...z...z...
```

Figure 5.1
Oh, stop. I can't stand it.

You know **Times-Roman** and Avant Garde
And **Bookman** and **Helvetica**;
Palatino and *Zapf Chancery*
And **New Century Schoolbook** and `Courier`;
But do you recall
The most famous typeface of all?

Figure 5.2
For real variety, you need something with real font capability.

Jargon alert: Postscript is a term you'll see used in connection with any standard font discussion. Postscript is actually the name of a special language used to communicate text descriptions to the printer. Some laser printers are Postscript printers, and some are PCL printers, which use a different kind of language.

Where Do They Come From?

Fonts come from the far-away land of Fontanel, where they float around in the ozone until a stork with a drinking problem grabs them in a little handkerchief...wait, wrong story.

Printers with font talent come with fonts already loaded. Postscript printers have 36 different fonts available right off the bat (Times Roman, New Century Schoolbook, Palatino, and a bunch of others you don't need to know unless you've got a Postscript printer). PCL printers also have their own variety of fonts, and, depending on the age of your printer, you may have a font cartridge to insert in a special slot. (Font cartridges went out of fashion about the same time as the S&L crisis, but I don't think the two were related.)

Today, you can purchase fonts from almost anyone standing on a street corner. Fonts are software, remember, so most computer retailers and software mail-order outlets carry packages of different fonts. You'll see lots of buzzwords when you start investigating font capabilities: bit mapped, TrueType, Adobe, the list goes on and on. We're going to leave the high-end font juggling for the experts and just learn to use the fonts we've already got.

WordPerfect sets a default font—that's the font used for all documents until you choose a different one—when you first install the program. You can change the default for the current document by setting the font (instructions are coming up) when you first open the document. If you want to change the default font forever and ever, press Ctrl-F8 to display the Font dialog box, press Shift-F1 to display the Font Setup dialog box, and press 1 to Select Initial Font.

Font Application: The Base Coat

Okay, so assuming that you can use different fonts (meaning that your printer can print them), how do you tell WordPerfect to change the font it's using?

First find out what font WordPerfect uses as the default. If you've already installed a printer (which you—or the person who installed WordPerfect for you—did during installation), the font WordPerfect uses as a matter of course is displayed in the bottom left corner of the screen, as shown in figure 5.3.

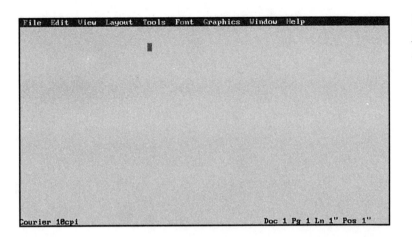

File Edit View Layout Tools Font Graphics Window Help

Courier 10cpi   Doc 1 Pg 1 Ln 1" Pos 1"

Figure 5.3

Find out what font is being used.

Here, Courier 10 is being used. Your screen might show something different. Don't sweat it.

You can change the font in one of two ways, depending on what you're doing:

■ If you're changing text you've already entered, you need to highlight the text first and then change the font.

■ If you're changing the font of text you're about to enter, you can turn that particular font on before you type.

Changing Already-Entered Text

To change the font of text you've already typed, first select the text you want to change. To select text, position the mouse at the beginning of the text and then press and hold the mouse button while dragging the mouse to the end of the area you want to change. This marks the text block you want to change. Figure 5.4 shows the highlighted block.

Now open the Font menu and choose the Font command. The Font dialog box appears, as shown in figure 5.5. To see what fonts are available for your printer, use the mouse to click on the down-arrow at the end of the Font line. A drop-down box appears, listing the fonts (see fig. 5.6). Click on the one you want, and WordPerfect enters it in the Font line. When you're finished changing settings, press Enter or click OK.

Figure 5.4
Selecting the text to change.

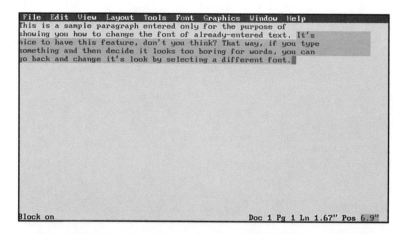

```
 File  Edit  View  Layout  Tools  Font  Graphics  Window  Help
This is a sample paragraph entered only for the purpose of
showing you how to change the font of already-entered text. It's
nice to have this feature, don't you think? That way, if you type
something and then decide it looks too boring for words, you can
go back and change it's look by selecting a different font.




Block on                                   Doc 1 Pg 1 Ln 1.67" Pos 6.9"
```

Figure 5.5
The Font fashion box.

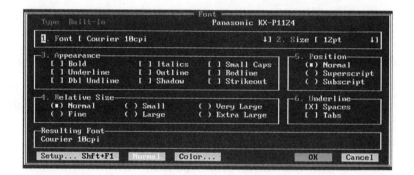

```
                           ─Font─
 Type  Built-In            Panasonic KX-P1124
 1. Font [ Courier 10cpi                        ↓] 2. Size [ 12pt        ↓]
 ─3. Appearance──────────────────────────────   ─5. Position───
   [ ] Bold          [ ] Italics   [ ] Small Caps  (■) Normal
   [ ] Underline     [ ] Outline   [ ] Redline     ( ) Superscript
   [ ] Dbl Undline   [ ] Shadow    [ ] Strikeout   ( ) Subscript
 ─4. Relative Size───────────────────────────   ─6. Underline──
   (■) Normal     ( ) Small     ( ) Very Large     [X] Spaces
   ( ) Fine       ( ) Large     ( ) Extra Large    [ ] Tabs
 ─Resulting Font─────────────────────────────────────────────
  Courier 10cpi

 Setup... Shft+F1   Normal   Color...              OK    Cancel
```

You can display the Font box without opening the menu and choosing
the command if you press Ctrl-F8.

New Text in a New Font

If you're getting ready to type a section of text and you want to change the
font of the stuff you're about to enter, you can bypass all that text-selection
nonsense and cut right to the chase. Just open the Font menu and choose
the Font command (or press Ctrl-F8). The Font dialog box appears, and you
can choose the font (and other settings) you want to use.

Figure 5.6
Look at all those choices!

Getting Stylish

Whether you want to admit it or not, we all want to look good in print. If we spend minutes, hours, or days with our words, we want them to represent us well when we're not around. The boss finds your memo on her desk three days after the board meeting and thinks "Hmmmm. This is a cool memo. I can tell this person went to a lot of trouble. I think I'll dig out the bonus sheet..."

Or does she look at the memo and think "Golly, this person is still living in the Dark Ages. Maybe I should bring in some fresh blood..."

It's something to think about, anyway. Going to that little extra trouble to spruce up your documents can be well worth your time. WordPerfect gives you several different fashions in which to wrap your text.

What Is a Text Style?

Unlike a font, which encompasses the typeface, style, and size of text, a text style is a single attribute that conveys the text's attitude. You'll use four basic styles most often in documents and others with more specialized uses. These styles are as follows:

- Normal
- **Bold**
- *Italic*
- <u>Underline</u>

That's the four basic. Now for the more specialized:

- <u>Double underline</u>
- Outline
- **Shadow**
- SMALL CAPS
- ~~Strikeout~~

Some people also lump two other attributes which are really "positions"—Superscript and Subscript—into the Style category. Superscript causes the characters to ride half a line higher (like H^2O), and subscript causes text to be half a line lower.

Why Use It?

Normal, do-nothing text is your everyday paragraph. There's nothing special—no shouting, no whispering, no *emphasis*. Bold is often used to state something strongly; to call attention to a necessary term or phrase.

Italic is the standard style used when terms are defined or when you lean on a word ("No, I *didn't* say that.")

If you're working with a printer that doesn't give you the option of choosing different fonts and using different sizes, you can still use styles to set off headings, important phrases, quotes, etc. Every printer will allow you to use boldface and italic, although not all printers can print the whole gamut of styles.

Style Application: Adding Pinash

Adding styles is simple. If you're adding a certain style to text that's already there, highlight the text (Remember how? Hint: Use the mouse.) and then open the Font menu (see fig. 5.7) and choose the style you want. The styles are listed starting with Bold and going through Strikeout. For the most often-used styles (Bold, Underline, and Italic), you can use the key combinations instead (F6, F8, and Ctrl-I, respectively).

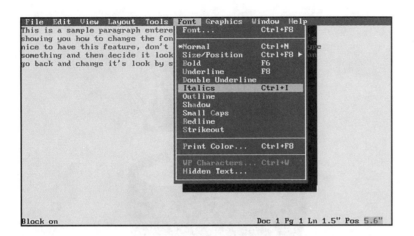

Figure 5.7
Applying a style.

To add a style to text you haven't entered yet, open the Font menu and select the style (or use the key combination) before you type. Using the key combination is much easier, like this:

1. Press F6.

2. Type This is bold text.

The text appears in bright white. It looks different from your other text, doesn't it? That's because WordPerfect has applied the bold style. When you want to turn off the bold attribute, press F6 again.

After you've built up your WordPerfect tolerance, you may want to try using WordPerfect styles to apply certain settings—such as font and formatting items—to your paragraphs. You create styles using the Styles option on the Layout menu. WordPerfect keeps track of the styles you create in a file called a stylesheet.

They're Out To Get Us

This is an area that is so ripe for problems that we could do an entire book just on font foibles. (Get out the Pepto Bismol.) We'll just cover a couple of the fixable common ones here.

Fickle Fonts

Okay, you highlighted your text; you opened the Font menu; and you chose the font you wanted to use. The status line on the bottom left side of the screen said you were using the font you wanted to use.

When you printed, your printer spit out boring, Courier, 10-point text. No eye-catching 12-point. No weenie 7.5-point. Why is WordPerfect teasing you?

First, your printer may not be able to print in different sizes. Check your printer's manual to be sure.

Second, did you install the right printer at print time? When you open the Font dialog box (by choosing Font from the Font menu), your printer's name should appear in the top right side of the box (see fig. 5.8). If a printer other than the one you are using is shown there (or if None selected appears), you need to change the printer setup to work with WordPerfect (or go out and buy the printer shown there, which isn't a real practical option).

Figure 5.8
Making sure that your printer is selected.

Changing the printer setup means running the installation program again (and if you didn't do it in the first place, this is going to scare your socks off). Better yet, find someone else to do it for you.

Not On *My* Screen, It Isn't!

So you decided to get a little stylish on us, huh? You created a potpourri of special effects, determined to get our attention. But where's the bold? The italic? The book said you should see the stuff on-screen, and it's *not* there.

Where is it?

Not all computer systems are set up to work the same way, with the same colors and the same attributes. When you're working with WordPerfect's text mode (there are other modes called Graphics mode and Page mode, which you may have trouble using if you don't have enough memory), the text styles are distinguished on the screen, but they don't necessarily appear the way they will in print.

Boldface, on most monitors, appears as bright white text. Italics appear as yellow, and underlined text is blocked in a white highlight.

Nothing Works!

Oh, I know the feeling. There's a great deal of teeth gnashing going on, isn't there? You're clutching the arms of your chair, trying to restrain yourself from beating the computer to death.

If you're trying to use fonts, and everything is really screwy, you may need to do something that you probably should have done in the first place (or, at least, someone who knows should have done it first): set up your fonts.

Some printers have fonts built right in, and that's that. No mess, no fuss. Sometimes, however, you need to set up fonts to be used with both WordPerfect and with your printer. Doing this involves the use of a separate utility—the WordPerfect Font Installer—that you get to from within the Font dialog box.

When the Font dialog box is displayed, press Shift-F1. The Font Setup dialog box appears, as shown in figure 5.9. Changing the settings in this box is not for the faint-hearted, and you should probably enlist the help of some font-literate person before proceeding. Within this dialog box, you can set the default font (remember that?), choose graphics fonts, tell WordPerfect whether you're using cartridges (remember those?), and set a number of other options. The biggie, however, is the Install Fonts option, number 9. When you select that option, you are taken to the Font Installer so that you can tell WordPerfect all about the fonts you want to use in your documents.

Figure 5.9
*Please don't make
me do this!*

If you're the type of person who enjoys struggling with the Rubik's cube, you'll like working with fonts. Otherwise, get the Excedrin.

Demon-Strations

Fontasy On-Screen (with Apologies to Fantasy On Ice)

1. Position the cursor at the beginning of the text for which you want to change the font.

2. Press and hold down the mouse button.

3. Drag the mouse to the end of the text you want to change.

4. Release the mouse button.

5. Open the Font menu by pointing to it and clicking the mouse button (or by pressing Alt-F).

6. Choose the Font command. The Font dialog box appears.

7. Click on the down arrow at the end of the Font line. A drop-down list of fonts appears.

8. Click on the font you want to use or highlight it and press Enter.

9. After setting the font, click OK or press Enter.

Stylish, Yet Functional, Too

1. On a blank line, press F6.

2. Type *This is bold text.*

3. Press F6 again.

4. Type *this is normal text.*

5. Press F8.

6. Type *this is underlined text.*

7. Press F8 again.

8. Type *this is normal text.*

9. Press Ctrl+I

10. Type *this is italic text.*

11. Press Ctrl+I again.

12. Type *this is normal text.*

Ha! Good job. You now have settled into the rhythm of using text styles. Figure 5.10 shows you what you've just done.

Figure 5.10
Playing with text styles.

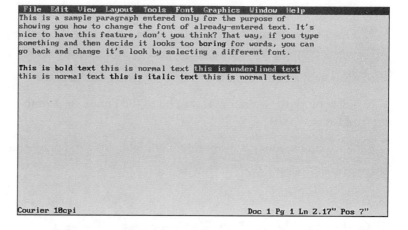

```
 File  Edit  View  Layout  Tools  Font  Graphics  Window  Help
This is a sample paragraph entered only for the purpose of
showing you how to change the font of already-entered text. It's
nice to have this feature, don't you think? That way, if you type
something and then decide it looks too boring for words, you can
go back and change it's look by selecting a different font.

This is bold text this is normal text this is underlined text
this is normal text this is italic text this is normal text.




Courier 10cpi                              Doc 1 Pg 1 Ln 2.17" Pos 7"
```

Summary

This encounter has included some of the basics for changing the look of your text. It may be something you won't want to tackle right away, or you may be juggling fonts from the start. Fonts control the overall look of the characters—typeface, style, and size. The text's style is like the text's attitude. You can make your text shout, whisper, whine, joke, or plead. (*Please, please,* let this encounter be over!)

Exorcises

1. What's a font? _____

    a. A short name for fountain.

    b. Something other people envy.

    c. A typographical term for a typeface, style, and size.

    d. A baby's soft spot.

2. Give two examples of a font.

3. What characteristics are included in a font?

4. Name four basic text styles.

5. What's the first step in changing the font or style of already entered text?

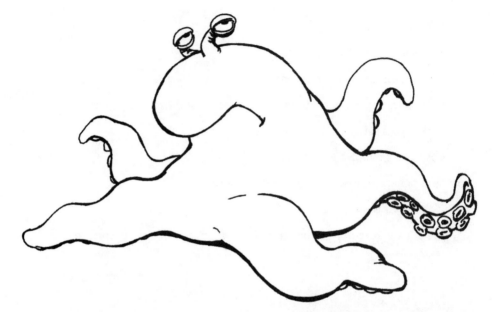

6th Encounter

This Tab's for You: Simple Formatting

Goal

To help you learn some quick-and-easy formatting techniques using our friend, the Tab key.

What You Will Need

WordPerfect (or a reasonable facsimile) and a Tab key (preferably still attached to the keyboard).

Terms of Enfearment

Left tab	Right tab
Center tab	Decimal tab
tab stops	monospaced fonts
proportional fonts	

Briefing

Tabs are not something to fear. Seemingly cryptic, ever mysterious, the tab provides an atmosphere of wonder and awe. How does the cursor know to move that number of spaces? How do all those lines magically line up with a simple press of a single key?

The tab can make your life oh-so-much easier than it is right now. Office a mess? Push the Tab key and watch your papers file themselves in order. See your books close up and align themselves along the edge of your desk.

Sold? Let's get busy.

Do I Have To Use Tabs?

Are you whining again? No, of course you don't have to use tabs. In fact, you can type text into your document and try—over and over again—to use the spacebar to line everything up. (Or you can forget about trying to line everything up, but your client's won't be very impressed—and your boss will be less so.)

Perhaps you don't understand the importance of the tab stop. A little enlightenment will help.

The tab helps you align text in your documents. Suppose, for example, that you are working on a letter similar to the one shown in figure 6.1. If you press the spacebar, you might be able to line up the column of goodies (although we're not recommending it).

But what happens if you want to add a second column beside the first? That second column is going to be out of alignment, unless you use a tab stop. Why? Because unless you're using a *monospaced font*—a font in which all the letters take up exactly the same amount of space—you're going to have unequal amounts of space given to the different letters. Thinner letters take up less room than wider letters. An "l" can slip in spaces that would be impossible for a W (without NutriSystem, anyway). These fonts, in which letters take up different amounts of space depending on their widths, are called *proportional fonts.* Because of proportional fonts, your tables will look horrible if you don't use tabs.

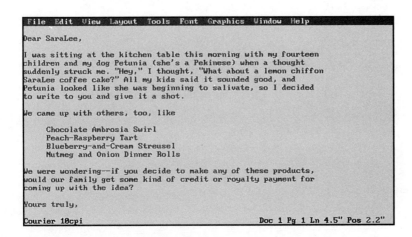

Figure 6.1
Your columns need tab stops.

Tabs and Taboos

Okay, so you know it's a no-no to use spaces when you should be using tabs. Are you clear on why? Because text that you want to look like this:

Product	Secret Recipe Code
Lemon Chiffon	B1
Choc/Ambrosia Swrl	A5
Peach/Rasp Tart	F2
Blueb/Cream Strsl	C7
Nutmeg/Onion	A3

Could wind up looking like this when you print:

Product	Secret Recipe Code
Lemon Chiffon	B1
Choc/Ambrosia Swrl	A5
Peach/Rasp Tart	F2
Blueb/Cream Strsl	C7
Nutmeg/Onion	A3

And we *know* you don't want that.

WordPerfect gives you four different types of tabs you can use in your documents:

- Left tabs
- Right tabs
- Center tabs
- Decimal tabs

Lefties

When you stick a left tab in your document, the text lines up along the left edge. The tabbed text in figure 6.1 shows text lined up on a left tab, for example.

Left tabs are the default, meaning that when you set a tab, it's a left tab, unless you specify otherwise.

Far and away, you'll use left tabs more often than anything else.

Rightwingers

You'd expect right tabs to be more conservative than their left counterparts, but not so. Right tabs are more unusual and used primarily for artistic purposes, such as when you're trying to line up text around a piece of art. When you set a right tab, text that is tabbed to that point is lined up along the right edge. (Think about it—not something you see often.)

Figure 6.2 shows how the product list looks if it is lined up along a right tab.

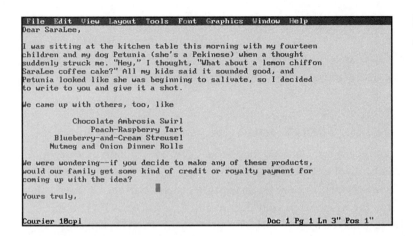

Figure 6.2
Pastry on the right.

Middle of the Road

Another kind of tab WordPerfect offers is the center tab. This guy really comes in handy when you want to center headings or create special effects (like centering all the entries on a fancy-shmancy menu).

The centered tab turns your ordinary text into Something Special, as shown in figure 6.3.

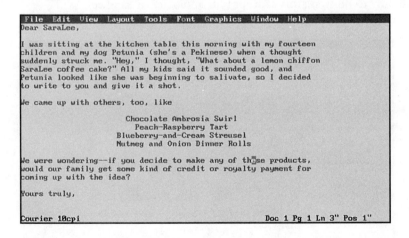

Figure 6.3
Your words—center stage.

Okay, so I'm beating some flat pastry, but think about how difficult it would be to accurately center all those different lines of text with the spacebar. You'd do it once, print it, find out it's out of whack. Do it again, print it, see that you overcompensated. Do it *again*....(Come back later. I'll be here a while.)

To the Point, Aren't You?

The final tab type is one that you may or may not use regularly: the decimal tab. Do you find yourself sneaking numbers into documents on a regular basis? Do you repeatedly quote financial strategems and projected sales increases? Do the numbers in your documents appear to crawl across the page all by themselves?

The decimal tab helps you line it all up. Come out of the financial closet and admit it: you're a numbers person. You like them. They make you happy.

With WordPerfect, you can use numbers in your document to your heart's content. And they never have to look less than wonderful again, all because of a little decimal tab.

To illustrate the decimal tab, we've added a second column to the sample letter (see fig. 6.4). The column, actually, means absolutely nothing and is included only to illustrate this concept (our apologies to SaraLee).

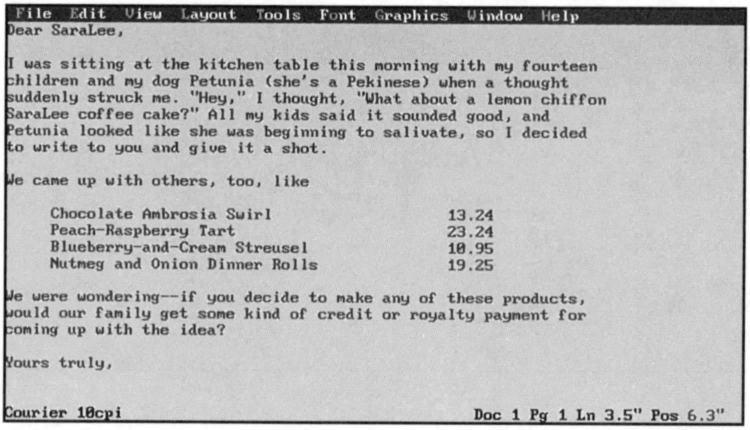

Figure 6.4
*Cross this dot—
I dare you.*

```
 File  Edit  View  Layout  Tools  Font  Graphics  Window  Help
Dear SaraLee,

I was sitting at the kitchen table this morning with my fourteen
children and my dog Petunia (she's a Pekinese) when a thought
suddenly struck me. "Hey," I thought, "What about a lemon chiffon
SaraLee coffee cake?" All my kids said it sounded good, and
Petunia looked like she was beginning to salivate, so I decided
to write to you and give it a shot.

We came up with others, too, like

     Chocolate Ambrosia Swirl                    13.24
     Peach-Raspberry Tart                        23.24
     Blueberry-and-Cream Streusel                10.95
     Nutmeg and Onion Dinner Rolls               19.25

We were wondering--if you decide to make any of these products,
would our family get some kind of credit or royalty payment for
coming up with the idea?

Yours truly,

Courier 10cpi                              Doc 1 Pg 1 Ln 3.5" Pos 6.3"
```

Hanging Out at the Tab Stop Cafe

Working with tabs is about as simple as anything in WordPerfect ever is. You can set tabs for text that's already there, and you can set tabs for text you haven't entered yet. You can also delete single tabs or wipe them all away. You can easily change tabs from one type to another (for example, you could change a left tab to a center tab) and include dot leaders (those little dots that stretch from the edge of your text to the number) if you chose.

WordPerfect already includes tabs—set for you—at every half-inch across the page. You may never have to mess with those tabs at all. How do you use the tabs already there? Press the Tab key! (Feel pretty silly, don't you?)

> **It's Time for Tab Jeopardy!** The answer for $100: Press either the Backspace key or Shift+Tab. The question is "How do you move the cursor backward one tab?"

Climbing Up on the Tab Set Box

You'll work with the tabs you set, specify, and clear in the Tabs Set dialog box. If you're adding tabs to text already entered, highlight the text you want to use. If you want to add tabs for text you're about to enter, place the cursor on a blank line. Then open the Layout menu and choose the Tab Set command. The Tab Set dialog box appears (see fig. 6.5).

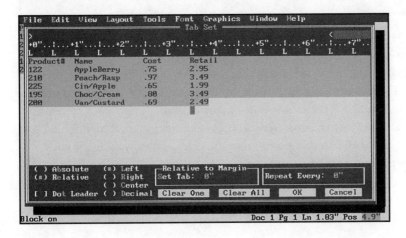

Figure 6.5

There's a whole lot of Tab-settin' goin' on.

Clearing Tabs

For best results, before you add your own tabs, clear the ones that are already there. (It makes working with your own less confusing.)

To clear tabs, click on the Clear All button in the bottom of the Tab Set dialog box. After you click the button, WordPerfect wipes away all the tabs and scrunches your text together (see fig. 6.6).

Figure 6.6
Hey! You call that helping?

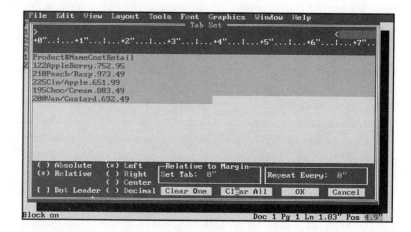

It's Time for Double Tab Jeopardy! The answer for $200: Click on the Clear One button. And the question is: "How do you get rid of only one tab in the tab line?"

Adding Tabs

Putting tabs back in is as easy as taking them out. Now, all you have to do is position the mouse cursor at the point on the ruler bar where you want to add the tab and click the mouse button. For example, we're going to put the first tab at the one-inch mark (see fig. 6.7). The ruler mark is highlighted, and the cursor beneath that position on the ruler blinks, waiting for you to choose what type of tab you want.

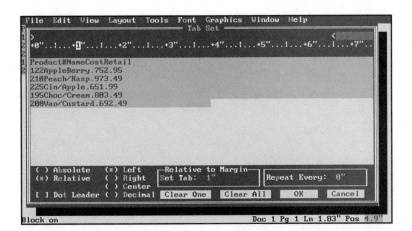

Figure 6.7
Always clean up your own mess.

To choose the tab type, click on the appropriate tab in the bottom of the Tab Set dialog box. This first tab should be a left one, so click Left. An L is placed in the tab line beneath the ruler, and the second column of text is moved over to the tab (see fig. 6.8).

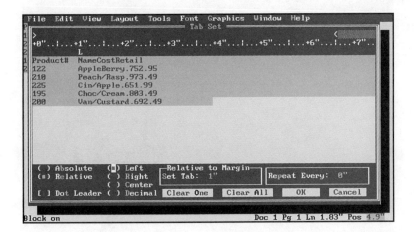

Figure 6.8
See? It already looks better, doesn't it?

Now you can add the next two in the same way, except these two should be decimal tabs (so their little points align). Position the mouse pointer on the three-inch mark and click; then click Decimal. Finally, click beneath the four-inch mark and click Decimal. All the columns should align as shown in figure 6.9.

Figure 6.9
*All done. Wasn't so
bad, right?*

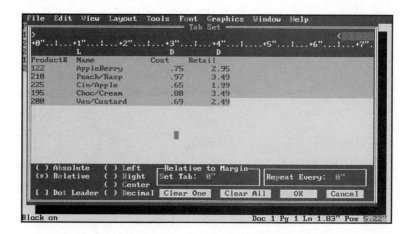

```
 File  Edit  View  Layout  Tools  Font  Graphics  Window  Help
                              Tab Set
 >                                                          <
 +0"..!...+1"...!...+2"...!...+3"...!...+4"...!...+5"...!...+6"...!...+7".
          L            D         D
 Product#  Name         Cost      Retail
 122       AppleBerry      .75      2.95
 210       Peach/Rasp      .97      3.49
 225       Cin/Apple       .65      1.99
 195       Choc/Cream      .80      3.49
 200       Van/Custard     .69      2.49



 ( ) Absolute   ( ) Left   ─Relative to Margin─
 (*) Relative   ( ) Right  Set Tab:  0"        │ Repeat Every:   0" │
                ( ) Center
 [ ] Dot Leader ( ) Decimal │Clear One│ │Clear All│  │  OK  │ │Cancel│
 Block on                              Doc 1 Pg 1 Ln 1.83" Pos 5.22"
```

If you want to add a dot leader (those little dots between text and page numbers in a table of contents), just click on the Dot Leader option in the Tab Set dialog box when you add a tab. (It's *my* turn to be the dot leader! I *never* get to be the dot leader! *Mom*!)

They're Out To Get Us

There are lots of little subtleties and nuances involved in getting the most out of your tabs. You'll get the hang of it. Just takes a little practice.

The first time you try to format some supremely complicated table, you'll fuss and fume and swear a bit. After that, everything will start to fall into place. (Ahhh... it's all becoming clear to me now...)

> **It's Time for Final Tab Jeopardy!** The answer for the championship is: A relative tab is measured from the left margin, and an absolute tab is measured from the left edge of the page. What's the question? You have 60 seconds. *Do dee do dee do dee dooo...*

Tab Misbehavin'

Even the most guru-ish word processing extraordinaire has trouble with tabs now and then. Things may look okay on-screen, but when you highlight that text and it appears in the Tab Set box, things are goofed up. The third column is stuck over where the fourth column should be—except the heading, which is in the right place.

What the heck is going on?

Sometimes, it's tempting to push the old Tab key one too many times when you're working in the regular document. You might not even realize you're doing it. One word is short, so you press Tab twice so that the columns line up on-screen. But then when you go to apply the Tabs, WordPerfect bumps everything over too far.

Lost? Here's an example:

WordPerfect puts tabs every half inch, like this:

Tab	*Tab*	*Tab*	*Tab*	*Tab*
1	1	1	1	1
22	22	22	22	22
333	333	333	333	333
4444	4444	4444	4444	4444
55555	55555	55555		

See what happened? The final entry (55555) is too wide to fit in a single column, so we pressed Tab only three times. When you look at this table in the Tab Set box, all other rows will have the right number of entries, but the last one will have only three. The moral? Make sure that you press Tab only once between each column entry. Then when you add Real Tabs, everything will line up.

Outta Whack Heads*

*Sung to the tune of Jimmy Cracked Corn (which I never understood either).

So you go to all this trouble to get the darned table lined up with its left tabs and decimal tabs, and you think you're done, when the column headings end up looking ridiculous. Oh, sure, that's professional. Nicely aligned decimal tabs, with the column headings hanging out (see fig. 6.10).

The best way to fix this is to set two different tab lines: one for the headings, and one for the meat of the table. When you set the tab line for the headings, make the tabs at 3 and 4 inches center tabs instead of decimal tabs (see fig. 6.11). That'll fit it.

Today's Answer to Final Tab Jeopardy: The question is "What is the difference between an absolute tab and a relative tab?" (No, sorry, an uncle with a bar bill doesn't qualify.)

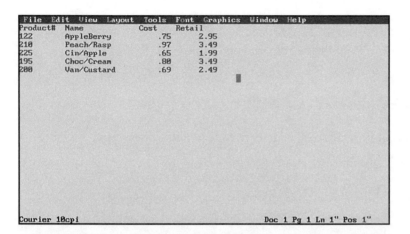

Figure 6.10
Funky column heads.

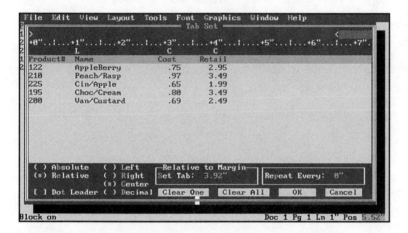

Figure 6.11
Putting heads in their place.

Demon-Strations

Swatting Tabs

Let's get rid of those extra tabs. Oh, come on—you remember how:

1. Highlight the text you want to change.

2. Open the Layout menu.

3. Choose the Tab Set command.

4. In the Tab Set dialog box, click the Clear All button.

Grow Your Own

To add your own tabs to already entered text, follow these steps:

1. Highlight the text.

2. Open the Layout menu.

3. Choose Tab Set. (See a pattern here?)

4. Click on the ruler line to indicate where you want the tab.

5. Select the tab type you want (Left, Right, Center, or Decimal) from the options on the bottom of the screen.

6. Specify whether you want the tab to be absolute or relative and whether you want dot leaders.

Repeat for any additional tabs or until you've lost between three and five pounds.

Summary

This encounter has taken you face to face with one of the most hated of the formatting creatures: tabs. We've met the enemy, and they is us.

Tabs really and truly make life easier, and using them in WordPerfect is no more complicated than anything else. Just practice a little; you'll get it. And if you can make your mistakes on someone *else's* file, even better.

Exorcises

1. Name the four popular tab types.

2. Explain why you might use a tab in a document. (Or if you wouldn't, why someone else might.)

3. Complete this sentence: A tab is to a document as a dog is to a _____.

4. Before you add your own tabs, you might want to _____.

   a. Turn on the computer.

   b. Remove the tabs WordPerfect set for you.

   c. Finish your coffee.

   d. Try moving one on your own.

5. True or false: After you've set tabs for a section of text, you can't reset them.

Much Ado about Printing

Goal

To help alleviate any printer anxiety you may be feeling.

What You Will Need

Your copy of WordPerfect loaded; a file you'd like to print (or a screen with a few lines of nonsense); a printer connected to the system and ready to rock.

Terms of Enfearment

preview	print options
initialization	soft fonts
print range	graphics fonts

Briefing

Whether or not you admit it, printing is truly the *coup-de-grace* of word processing. Why else would you take all that time to enter text, format it, make sure that the spelling is right, and perform other brain-numbing tasks, if you never intended to print the thing?

Of course you did.

Have you heard that printing is one of those unavoidable trouble spots you can accidentally fall into on your way to the land of Finished Documents? Some people have more trouble with printing than others. If you're trying to do a simple printout with regular paper, no fancy fonts (remember them?), and no complicated formats—in other words, you're printing a memo—you should be all right. But printing an elaborate document with columns, graphics, various fonts, lines, headers, and footers is just asking for trouble. Don't expect to get out of that print job without throbbing temples. At least the first time.

But that's the nature of all word processing programs, not WordPerfect in particular. Printing is supposed to be something like childbirth: by the time you get the document just the way you want it, you know you've done something significant. There's that feeling of accomplishment that just might not be there if things were too easy.

Well, maybe.

Taking a Little Look-See

Font flashback: In Encounter 6, you learned that there are monospaced fonts and proportional fonts. In monospaced fonts, all the characters take up the same amount of space (an l gets the same width as a w). In proportional fonts, the letters are given space according to what they need, so the letter t would get less space than an M.

The font you see on the WordPerfect screen in text mode (which is the only mode you've see so far) is not the same as the fonts you'll use in the finished document. That means that your printout may be quite a bit different from the text you see on-screen, which means that you need some way of seeing what you're going to print before you print it. Just so there are no surprises at print time.

[Cue: Leave It To Beaver music.]

Ward and June Cleaver Present: Preview

Introducing Preview, the WordPerfect feature that allows you to see what's coming before it hits. Avoid those shaky moments by the printer output tray. Relax in the comfort of your own office, secure in the knowledge that things are as they are supposed to be.

Preview. By WordPerfect.

You can get to preview in one of two ways:

■ You can open the File menu and choose Print Preview (see fig. 7.1).

■ You can select the Print command from the File menu and, from the Print Options dialog box, choose Print Preview (see fig. 7.2).

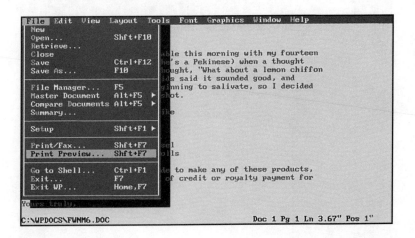

Figure 7.1
Print Preview—the quick way.

Figure 7.2
*Last minute preview
in the Print/Fax box.*

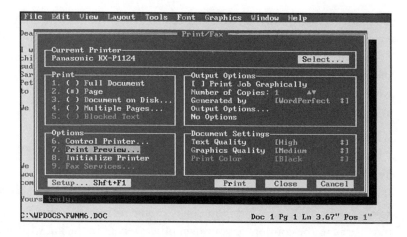

Like Ward and June, Preview displays in black and white (see fig. 7.3). That doesn't lessen the effectiveness of the display, however. Look at that pleasant Button Bar (cute name). Notice the easy-to-use pull-down menus on the top left. You easily can select a variety of ways to see your document—you can zoom in or out, display thumbnail pictures, and make choices about the display.

Figure 7.3
*One good preview is
worth a thousand
bad prints.*

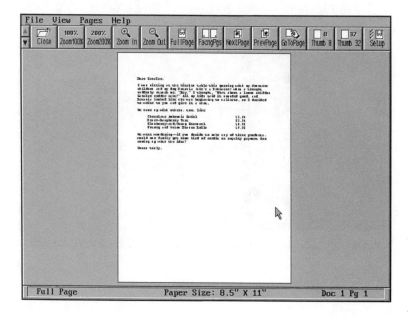

Rules for Good Previews

Golly gee, Wally—how're we gonna remember all this stuff?

- Display the document you want to see before selecting Print Preview.

- Position the cursor at the top of page 1 before printing; or, if you want to see a specific page, place the cursor on that page before choosing Preview. (If you forget, no big deal. You can move from page to page easily within Preview.)

- Use the different views to check out the typeface, styles, and formatting of your words. You can choose from real-life size, magnified (two times normal view), reduced, two-page, and thumbnail views.

- Always make sure that you sit at least three feet back from the television screen.

- Don't get discouraged when you find out that you can't edit anything in preview. (That's why it's called *preview* mode—not preview-and-edit mode.)

- Escape from preview by opening the File menu and choosing the Close command or by clicking the Close button.

You're the One, Babe—Selecting a Printer

Another important pre-printing step involves making sure that you've selected a printer. Have you?

That usually happens during program installation. If you didn't install WordPerfect yourself and have no idea whether a printer was installed, you can check by pressing Shift+F7 when you have a document open on the screen. The Print/Fax dialog box appears (it's the same box that you saw in figure 7.2). If a printer is selected, the name of the printer is shown in the Current Printer area at the top of the Print/Fax box (see fig 7.4).

Figure 7.4
Make sure that the printer is selected.

This is the
selected
printer.

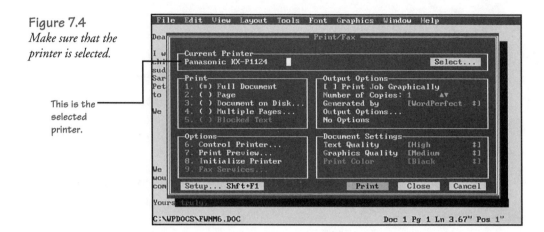

What? No printer is selected? Well, quick, before anybody notices, click the Select button. The Select Printer screen appears, showing you the possible printers you can select (see fig. 7.5).

Figure 7.5
Finding your print-mate.

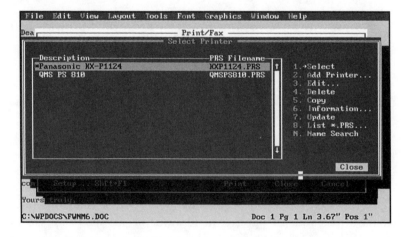

Notice that this screen shows only two printers—the Panasonic (that's the dot matrix) and the QMS (the Postscript laser printer). There are only two shown here because I have only two PC printers. Your department or business may have many more printers available in the Select Printers screen.

Font Worries

I know what you're thinking: Oh, jeez, Edith, do we have to talk about fonts again?

Well, sorry, Archie, but fonts are part of WordPerfect life.

Fonts don't do you much good if the only place you see them is on-screen. Oh, sure, they look great in preview mode, but when you print all you get is page after page of Courier (which is known to cause heart disease in laboratory rats).

As mentioned in the last encounter, some printers have fonts built right in. More than a convenience issue, these printers can print a variety of fonts and sizes, and you just plain don't have to worry about it. Heaven.

But there are those of us who inherited our printers (and so can blame our headaches on someone else) who don't have those nifty built-in fonts and have to do something to send the fonts—remember, fonts are computer instructions—to the printer so that the printer knows what the heck to do.

> *Jargon alert:* Fonts that you purchase as software and then have to send to the printer at print time are called *soft fonts*. Just thought you'd want to know.

That something is called *downloading*. You download a font to the printer at print time so that the printer knows how to print the font you want to use. Get it?

WordPerfect will download your fonts for you, but WordPerfect wants to call it *initializing*, as in initializing the printer. To initialize the printer, display the Print/Fax menu (by opening the File menu and choosing Print/Fax or by pressing Shift+F7). Then press 8 or choose Initialize Printer. A little pop-up box gets in your face telling you the oh-so-important rules for initializing your friend the printer. After you press Enter or click OK, the computer chugs for a moment (you can just feel those little fonts running through the print cable to the printer) and then returns you to your open document.

Could we *please* stop talking about fonts now, Edith?

Oh, the Options of It All!

And you thought we were almost done, right? We're just getting started. You saw how many other things there were to worry about in the Print/Fax box. Let's take a look at it again, shall we? (Go ahead—look at figure 7.6.)

Figure 7.6

The Print/Fax dialog box—an encore presentation.

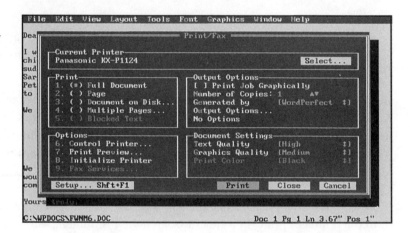

Let's just lump it all together before we lose half our audience to attention deficit disorder (or hunger pains): The rest of the printer options may concern you only once in a blue moon. You'll be laying in bed late on a Sunday night, stressing about the report you have to print in time for the 8:30 a.m. Monday meeting. You look out the window, trying to remember which WordPerfect print options are which, and you see...sure enough...the blue moon.

In the Print box on the Print/Fax dialog box, you see your typical print options. Do you want to print the whole thing? A single page? How about just a few pages, a booklet, or labels? The final option, Blocked Text, is selectable only if you highlighted a section of text before you displayed the dialog box.

The Output Options box lets you set things like the number of copies you want to print and how you want your printer to behave. WordPerfect will tell your printer to sort the printed pages, to collate them, or to lump them together, but there's a catch: your printer must be capable of doing those things before the process will work. The printer won't just oblige you because WordPerfect told it to. One special option in this group is Print Job Graphically, which will concern you only if you're printing art images that include light items printed on top of dark ones (and how often does *that* happen?).

Just Print It!

Aren't you tired of all this hullabaloo? Let's just print the darned thing.

There's one good side to all this printing fuss, however; by clicking the Setup button or pressing Shift+F1 when the Print/Fax dialog box is displayed, you can set all these print options for future generations of printed documents. All the documents you create from this moment on will grow up having these same preset print options. (You can change them at any time in the Print/Fax dialog box.) When you click the Setup button, the Print Setup dialog box appears (see fig. 7.7). That's where you choose the options for future documents.

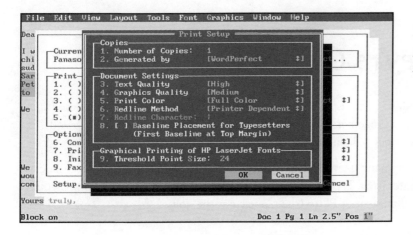

Figure 7.7

Saving print options for posterity (and future prints).

One final consideration: What quality do you want? Obviously, for final work—things that other people are going to see—you want the highest quality possible. For quick prints like rough drafts, you might want to choose Draft or Medium quality for Text and Graphics Quality.

When you're all done, click Print. (Whew!)

And keep your fingers crossed.

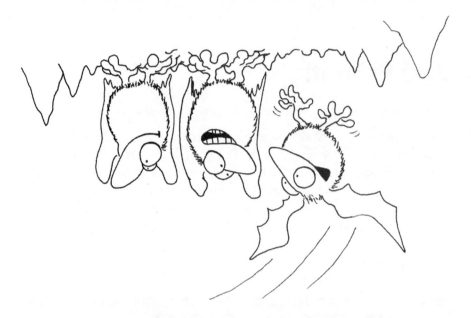

They're Out To Get Us

Oh, bad, bad printer. Cruel printer. You can do this to me after all the time we've spent together? After all the trouble I've gone through to keep you dusted, paper-fed, and inked up?

There are many, many things that can botch up your printing. It could be the printer itself. It could be fonts. It could be the cable connection. It could be the alignment of Pluto (the planet, not the dog).

Nothing, Nada, No Way

Well, guess what happened? Nothing is a good guess. The computer thought it was printing. You heard that tell-tale chunking. But the printer sat there, dormant.

Let's whittle the possibilities down one by one:

- Is the printer turned on?

- Is the printer cable connected to your system?

- Is the printer light on, showing that the printer is on line? (That means ready to receive information.)

- Did you initialize the printer? (Although this shouldn't keep the thing from printing altogether—it just keeps the printer from printing in the right font.)

- Was your printer selected in the Print/Fax box?

- Are you sure that you clicked the Print button and not the Cancel button?

Well, we had to ask.

Not an Option

Yeah, right. Selecting a printer is as easy as clicking on that Select button, huh? Well what if you don't have any printers listed in the Select Printers box? None. Nada.

Now what?

The reason you don't see any printers is that no printers were installed during installation. In order to set up a printer to work with WordPerfect, you're going to have to get out your program disks. Put the disk labeled Install 1 into either drive A or drive B (depending on which you need to use to match the size of the disk). Then (assuming that you're using drive B), type

> b:install

and press Enter. If the disk is in drive A, type

> a:install

and press Enter. After a second, the WordPerfect installation utility starts up. First the program asks you whether you see colors before your eyes. Answer honestly.

Next, you see a screen that lets you choose the kind of installation you want. The program is already installed, so you don't need to reinstall it. What you want is number 4, under Miscellaneous Options. This will allow you to update the printer installation (which, in your case, hasn't happened yet).

Now just follow the prompts along the path to printer installation. If at any time it gets just too scary for you, press Esc and Y to exit the installation. Then have someone who *likes* to do such things give you a hand.

Demon-Strations

Coming Attractions

1. Display the document you want to preview.

2. Open the File menu and choose Print Preview.

3. Change the Preview view by clicking the buttons in the Button Bar. (You can use the commands in the View menu, if you prefer.)

4. When you're finished previewing, open the File menu and choose Close or click on the Close button in the Button Bar.

Where's the Shredder?

1. Display the document you want to print.

2. Press Shift+F7 to display the Print/Fax box.

3. Select any necessary print options.

4. Select Print Preview, if you want.

5. If you need to download soft fonts, select Initialize Printer.

6. Specify the number of copies.

7. Click the Print button.

Summary

Well, aren't you proud of yourself? You've learned to sneak a peak at your document before you print and hopefully—did having your fingers crossed help?—you've been able to actually print your work. Exhilarating, isn't it? The next encounter explains the ins and outs of the Save command and covers a hodge-podge of important file and program tasks.

Exorcises

1. Explain monospaced and proportional fonts. (If you have to look it up, take away two points—and shame on you.)

2. What's the primary benefit of Preview?

    a. It tells you what movies are going to be on tomorrow night.

    b. It allows you to see how the document will look before you go to the trouble to print it.

    c. It saves paper (and innocent trees) by displaying the page on the screen.

3. Put the following print steps in order:

_____ Specify the quality

_____ Display the document on the screen

_____ Choose Print/Fax

_____ Click Print

_____ Open the File menu

_____ Make sure that the printer is selected

_____ Choose the range of pages to print

_____ Choose the number of copies

_____ Select output options

_____ Initialize the printer, if necessary

4. What does downloading mean?

a. Shipping feather pillows.

b. Sending fonts to the printer.

c. Moving the printer to a point lower than the system unit.

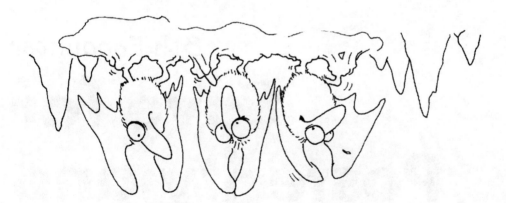

Save for Posterity and Exit, Stage Right!

Goal

To help you save those little jewels you create, reopen them, and leave WordPerfect altogether when you've had enough. (Wait! Don't go yet!)

What You Will Need

Nothing new here: WordPerfect loaded up, some text entered in a file (any text will do), and roughly 10 minutes.

Terms of Enfearment

directory	path
File Manager	Save As
autosave	

Briefing

You've already worked your way through quite a bit of the basic WordPerfect procedures (pause for back patting). You know how to create a document, edit and format it, change the font and style, and print it. We're forgetting something, though. If you don't save the file, all this fuss will have been for nothing.

Then, after you save your files, you've got to figure out how to open the files you created. WordPerfect gives you two different commands—Open and Retrieve—for doing just that. We explain which you should use and why in this encounter.

Finally, knowing how to exit WordPerfect is pretty necessary information: you can't just keep WordPerfect running all the time. (Well, *possible* but not *practical.*)

Save the Files

So, you've got a file open on the screen? Good.

Chances are, your files aren't close to extinction, and they aren't in danger from oil spills or tuna nets. And yet losing that one important file—the one you needed for this afternoon's meeting—is a Really Big Deal.

Saving your files is a practical necessity. Why else use a word processor, if you don't want to keep your files where you can use them again easily? Saving your files also safeguards you against the accidental loss of data. Most people—just to be safe—save their current file every 15 minutes or so.

When you save your file, WordPerfect writes the file (which at the time is being stored only in your computer's RAM, or temporary storage space) to a disk and saves it under a name you specify. The disk might be your hard disk or it might be a diskette in either drive A or B. The file lives there until you delete it, and you can reopen it, work on it, and resave it with your changes.

Nothing-Unusual Saves

Let's do a quick save. Ready?

The first time you save a file it takes a couple of seconds and keystrokes longer than subsequent saves, but it's nothing to gripe about.

First open the File menu and choose the Save command (or press Ctrl+F12) as shown in figure 8.1.

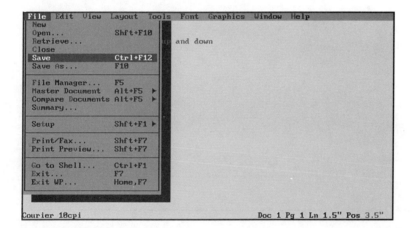

Figure 8.1
Get ready, set, save!

The Save Document 1 (that's the document you've got open on the screen, unless you've opened another document, and then it might be Document 2, or Document 3, or...) title appears at the top of the pop-up box (see fig. 8.2). You see a big rectangular box beside a little red Filename: label.

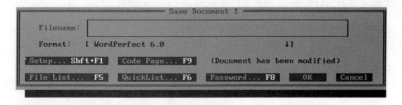

Figure 8.2
The Big Save.

Ready to save the file? Don't blink, or you might miss it.

Type a name for the file (something like POME1.DOC—short for po' little ol' me—or COOLSTUF.DOC). You can use up to eight characters for the part of the name before the period and three letters after. Then press Enter. You are dumped back to your document file, and the name of the file is now put in the bottom left corner of your document (see fig. 8.3).

Figure 8.3

Aren't you proud? A saved file.

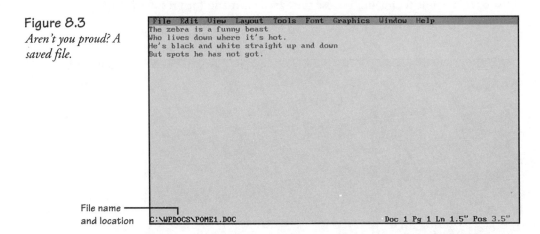

File name and location

After you save the file the first time, you can do a quick-save by simply pressing Ctrl+F12. WordPerfect doesn't bother asking you for the name or anything—it just saves the file, fast.

The Little Nuances of the Save Command

If you've got more time, you may want to investigate some of the options you have with your Save command. For example, you can do the following:

- Save the file in a format that can be used by other popular word processing programs (such as Ami Pro, Microsoft Word, and WordStar).

- Specify a different directory in which to store the file.

- Select a Fast Save (which writes the file to disk without any formatting code—which is quicker right now but may take longer at print time).

- Add a Password so that only you and Agent 99 can access the file.

- If you're working on a document in a different language (oh, *that* happens a lot), you can choose a code page (which saves the characters used in the document) to go along with the file.

After you have saved the file (like we just did with the fast save procedure), you can set these options by using the Save As command. As you'll notice, the Save As command is discussed in the next section, placed nearby for your convenience.

The Fabulous Save As Command

It's not uncommon to change your mind about things. So you didn't think about where you should store the file. You forgot that your officemate is still using WordPerfect 5 and needs your files formatted for her version. No biggie.

Save As to the rescue.

When you want to Save your file As something else (pretty cool, huh?), open the File menu and choose the Save As command (or you can press F10).

You see that same Save box you saw in the initial save. This time, you'll want to set some of the options. Here's how:

Choose a different format. If you want to select a different file, click on the down-arrow at the end of the Format box. A list of possible formats is displayed (see fig. 8.4). You can scroll through the list by clicking on the arrows at either end of the scroll bar. Click on the one you want, and WordPerfect puts that selection in the Format box.

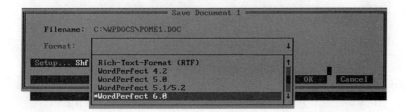

Figure 8.4
Formats R Us.

Setup the save. When you click the Setup button (or press Shift+F1), you can elect to use the Fast Save feature (remember that?) or choose a different default format in which all future files will be saved (unless you specify otherwise).

Choose a Code Page. Remember that special decoder ring that used to come in specially marked boxes of Lucky Charms? Well, that has nothing do to with Code Pages. A *Code Page*, cryptically enough, is a page that stores special characters used in a document written for another language. (If your word processing needs are that advanced, you're reading the wrong book.)

Using the File List. You use the File List when you want to save files in a certain directory by default. First press F5 or click the File List button. The Select List dialog appears (it's just a tiny little thing so we won't show it to you). Type the directory in which the file will be saved and click OK. Next, a File List dialog box appears, showing you the files in the directory you specified (see fig. 8.5). File List is really more useful when you're opening files, but you can select Use as Pattern to display the directory and even the filename (which you'll want to change slightly for subsequent files).

Figure 8.5

Wandering through the File list.

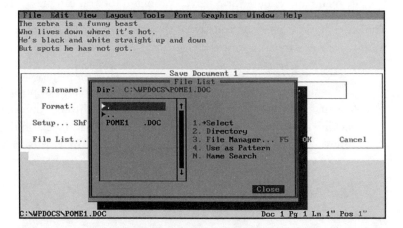

Quick, list! You can create a QuickList that displays directories and/or files you use often. For example, if you're always working in the

BRADY subdirectory, you can add that to a QuickList and have WordPerfect display it for you automatically. You click the QuickList button or press F5 to display the QuickList box; then use the options on the right to make your changes and additions.

Shhhh. What's the password? You can add a password to the file by pressing F8 or clicking on the Password button. The Password dialog box appears, in which you type the password of your choice (see fig. 8.6). Rules for passwords? Enter anything you want, in upper- or lowercase letters (it's all the same to WordPerfect). When you type, the cursor stays in the same place as though you're not typing anything (just in case someone from the KGB is looking over your shoulder). After you're done, click OK or press Enter. What's this? WordPerfect asks you to re-enter the password (just to make sure that you got it right—or to check that you're the same person you were a second ago). One more thing: Remember That Password! If you forget it, that file is as good as gone.

Figure 8.6
The mysterious invisible password.

Just like the traditional Save command, you complete Save As by clicking OK or pressing Enter. You also can click your heels three times and say, "There's No Place Like Guam, There's No Place Like Guam, There's No Place Like Guam."

Goodnight, Files

Hmmmm. You saved it, but there it is, still displayed on your monitor. How do you get rid of the darned thing? Oh, sure, you could open the File menu, select New, and start a new file right on top of this one, but something just seems messy about that.

If you've saved your file and are through with it, put the file away by opening the File menu and choosing the Close command. If you've made any changes to the file since the last time you saved it, WordPerfect will ask you whether you want to save the file. Answer the question as honestly as you can, and the file will close.

Opening Files

Now you know how to save your brainchildren. After you save the files, and they are tucked away safely in your WP60DOCS directory (which is where all good little files go to sleep), how do you wake them up again?

WordPerfect gives you two different commands—both neatly displayed in the File menu—that will open files: Open and Retrieve. This section explains them both.

Open, Retrieve, What's the Difference?

This is one of those things that, after you see the difference, you're going to say "Did they really have to make two separate commands for this?" Well, you and I don't understand all the esoteric purposes (or is that porpoises?) of such intellectually endowed programmers. Let's just believe it's for the best.

Put in as simple terms as possible, use Open when you want to work with a file you've saved to disk (either the hard disk or a diskette). You're opening a file, in other words.

Retrieve is the command of choice when you're working on a document and want to open another document into the one you're working on. Like when you're doing the quarterly report and want to include a document you wrote about the Popsicle of the Month. You retrieve the Popsicle article into your current document using Retrieve.

Oh, yes, we see it now. You definitely need two different commands for that.

Pandora's Rules for Successful Opening

The actual process for opening and retrieving is the same, though. Display the File menu and choose Open (or Retrieve). The Open Document dialog box appears (unless you chose Retrieve, and then the Retrieve Document dialog box appears). You can type the name of the file you want (don't forget the directory) in the `Filename:` box, or, if the file you want to open is one of the last four files you worked on, you can click the down-arrow in the right side of the `Filename:` box to display the most recently changed files (see fig. 8.7).

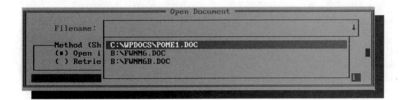

Figure 8.7
Opening, retrieving, whatever.

Highlight the file you want and press Enter. If a password has been assigned to the file, the Password box appears, waiting for you to enter the password.

Ooops!

Didn't forget it, did you? If so, you're sunk, plain and simple. Oh well. You learned a valuable lesson. Next time, name the file after something or someone you couldn't possibly forget, like Aunt Edna or your mother-in-law.

If you need to go looking for the file (it's not in the current directory), you can click the File Manager button or press F5. When the Specify File Manager List dialog box appears, you can type the name of the directory you want or use one of three find-it-quick options: QuickList, Use QuickFinder, or Directory Tree. The Directory Tree, shown in figure 8.8, shows you the various directories on your disk.

Figure 8.8
Treed again.

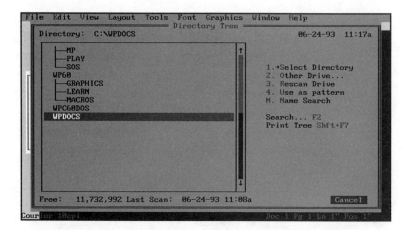

Time to Quit, WordPerfect

Oh, boy. Here we go again. Two commands that say Exit. (This is beginning to smack of governmental involvement.) Why are there *two*?

Actually, this time, these two Exits do different things. The bare Exit (all alone on a line in the File menu) actually closes the current file. (Which brings up something else—why have a Close command and an Exit command?)

Exiting the Normal Way

For best results (and better gas mileage), save your files before you exit WordPerfect. Foreseeing that this isn't always remembered, the makers of WordPerfect put a little safety net in there for you.

To exit WordPerfect, open the File menu and choose the Exit WP command (or press Home and then F7). The Exit WordPerfect dialog box appears, as shown in figure 8.9. If you've been working with only one open file, only one file is shown. In this figure, I've had three files open (you can open as many as nine at one time in WordPerfect 6).

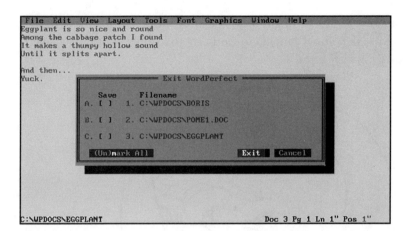

Figure 8.9
Mom, are we there yet?

If you want to save any of the displayed files, click in the open box in the Save column. Finally, press Enter or click the Save and Exit button. WordPerfect will then save and close those files for you and dump you back out to the DOS prompt.

> If you want to save all the files displayed in the Exit WordPerfect dialog box, you can click on the (Un)mark All button in the bottom left corner of the box. If all the files are unmarked, this marks them. If they are all marked, this unmarks them. Simple enough.

Exiting Wrong

There's an Exit WordPerfect command because the programmers know better than we do what happens to a file as it's being closed. It may look like we're done with it, and we may have already saved it, but saying "Oh, I'm finished," and shutting off computer power while WordPerfect is still on the screen is a Definite No-No.

You never know what might happen.(Little green men might come in the middle of the night and uninstall the program until you're responsible enough to care for it correctly.)

This abominable behavior might be tolerated by the program once or twice, but sooner or later, you'll come in to work, try to load up WordPerfect, and get a "Sorry Charlie" error.

They're Out To Get Us

Stand in the hallway outside the office of a new user, and you'll hear it, sooner or later:

"Where's my file?"

Although it seems, for the moment, that your computer has eaten the file, it is there, somewhere. Directories can be difficult things to deal with if you're unfamiliar with them.

When you save a file, WordPerfect puts it in a directory called WPDOCS automatically. You can change this directory to something else, if you want, but if you do, remember where you put the file.

When a file gets lost, there are only three possibilities:

- You didn't really save the file.

- You saved it in a directory different from your usual place.

- You accidentally deleted it.

Use the File Manager to look around for the misplaced file. (If you need help using the File Manager, see Encounter 18.)

Demon-Strations

Mother-May-I Save the File?

1. Open the File menu.

2. Choose the Save command.

3. Type a filename for the file.

4. Select a format, if necessary.

5. Use Setup to add Fast Save, if you want to.

6. Add a password, if you're working with sensitive stuff.

7. Click OK or press Enter.

Open Sesame

When you're ready to open a file, ask yourself whether you're opening a file you've already saved or whether you're incorporating a file into your current document. If you're opening a file, use Open. If you're adding a file to your current one, use Retrieve.

1. Open the File menu.

2. Choose either Open or Retrieve.

3. Type the directory and name of the file you want.

4. You can use the File Manager to display the directories on the hard disk, if you're not sure where the file you want is stored.

5. Click OK or press Enter.

So Long, WP!

1. Open the File menu.

2. Choose Exit WP.

3. When the Exit WordPerfect dialog box appears, click the open Save boxes if you want to save the file.

4. Click OK or press Enter.

Summary

You've learned quite a few important procedures in this encounter. Can't get by without saving; can't get by without opening; can't leave WordPerfect running forever. (Well, maybe...) This encounter rounds out Part I, completing the I've-Got-To-Do-This section. The next part introduces you to more specialized editing tasks—things you may or may not do as part of your daily WordPerfect routine.

Exorcises

1. What are the two different save commands? How are they different?

2. What's a Fast Save?

3. True or false: If you forget your password, you can exit to DOS, type PASSWORD, press Enter, and WordPerfect will display your password.

4. Explain the difference between Open and Retrieve.

5. True or false: You can exit WordPerfect by pressing F7.

The ABCs of Text Blocks

Goal

To help you learn how to grab the text you want to work with in what WordPerfect calls *text blocks*.

What You Will Need

You don't want to see it again: WordPerfect, a sample file, and some of those little plastic dinosaurs. (After you get your blocks assembled, you want to play with them, don't you?)

Terms of Enfearment

text blocks   marking
appending blocks   moving blocks

Briefing

In an earlier encounter, you learned the easiest of all editing techniques: the backspace key. There will be times, however, when you need to make changes on a larger scale. You need to move this paragraph over there; you need to add this sentence to that letter; you need to move this word to that sentence.

That's called block editing, which is what this encounter is all about.

New on the Block

What is a text block and why should you care? A text block can be as small as a single character or as large as the entire document. When you mark text as a block, you're saying to WordPerfect, "Here, this is what I want to move" (or copy, delete, or print). You'll mark text as a block before you do any of the following things:

- Copy text
- Move text
- Delete text
- Print a portion of text
- Put a pizza in the oven
- Change the font of selected text
- Change the way a section of text is formatted

Marking Text as a Block

How do you mark a block of text? You have different options, depending on whether you're using the keyboard or the mouse:

- Open the Edit menu and choose the Block command. The `Block on` message appears in the lower left corner of the screen. Use the arrow keys to move the highlight to include all the text you want (see fig. 9.1).

■ Use the mouse to point to the beginning of the block you want. Press and hold down the mouse button while dragging the mouse to the end of the text you want to highlight. Release the mouse button. The text is highlighted as a block.

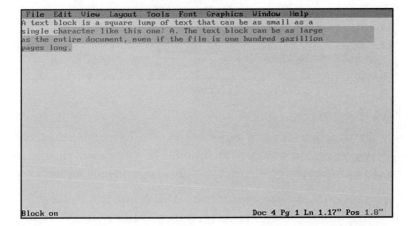

Figure 9.1
Blocking in progress.

You can use the Edit menu's Select command. When the cursor is positioned anywhere in the current document, open the Edit menu and choose Select. A submenu appears, giving you the option of selecting the paragraph in which the cursor is positioned, the current paragraph, or the entire page (see fig. 9.2). Click on your selection, and WordPerfect highlights the text.

Copying and Mooo-ving Blocks

Copying and moving text blocks is a routine operation that you'll perform on a fairly regular basis. If you're one of those people who writes in brain-dump fashion and then reorganizes your thoughts into some kind of logical progression (huh?), you'll like WordPerfect's easy-to-use copy and move procedures.

Figure 9.2

A different way to block.

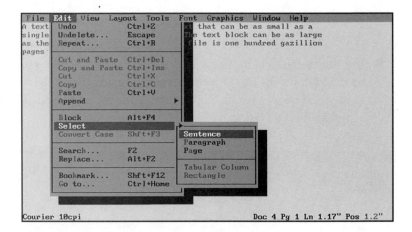

Say That Again?

When you want to make a copy of a section of text, start by marking the text you want to copy (remember how?). Next, open the Edit menu and choose Copy. (If you prefer, you can press Ctrl+C instead of opening the menu.)

After you make the copy, nothing appears to have happened. But secretly, behind the scenes, WordPerfect made a copy of the highlighted text and put it on the clipboard (an invisible storage area for text you're copying or moving).

To place the copy in the document (whether it's this document or another document), you have to use the Paste command, also in the Edit menu. Before you select Paste, however, position the cursor at the point you want the copied text to be inserted. After you select Paste, the text is put at the cursor position.

If you know that you want to copy and paste text in the same document, you can use the Copy and Paste command in the Edit menu. Highlight the text, choose the command, and then, as the message at the bottom of the screen says, move the cursor to the point where you want the text and press Enter.

Let's Put It Over There

Moving text isn't really moving text. What you're doing is cutting text from one place and putting it in another. When you move text, you have two options:

- You can select Cut, put the cursor where you want to insert the text and select Paste (both from the Edit menu).

- You can choose Cut and Paste from the Edit menu.

Similar to the Copy command, the Cut and Paste commands need you to highlight the text block first. If you're moving the text to a point within the document, you can use the Cut and Paste command.

Saving, Deleting, and Printing Blocks

Okay, we're cheating, lumping stuff like this all together in a single section. You don't want to read basically the same instructions over and over again, do you? (Not when you could be taking a Coke break; not when the Bulls are playing; not when you've got 101 more interesting things to do.)

Stack 'Em Up

Accumulating blocks? You bet. You can save the blocks you really like, the ones you would like to use as samples in your resume. How? Like this:

1. Select the block you want to save.

2. Open the File menu.

3. Choose the Save As command. The Save Block dialog box pops up (see fig. 9.3).

4. Enter a name for the block (how about *NewKids?*)

5. Press Enter or click OK.

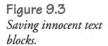

Figure 9.3
Saving innocent text blocks.

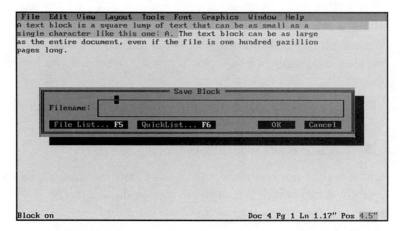

After the block is saved as a file, you can use the block in a file by using the Retrieve command to incorporate the saved block into your current document.

Throw Away Blocks

It happens. That text block just doesn't make any sense. You wish you hadn't written it. You are suddenly overcome with this murderous urge to delete it before anyone else sees it and makes fun of you. (Boy, can I sympathize.)

1. Mark your text.

2. Open the Edit menu.

3. Choose Cut.

That's it. No, really. Sure, it's part of a Cut and Paste operation, but in this case, you just don't ever Paste. The file floats around in File Purgatory forever and ever. Sound cruel? Not as cruel as your officemate getting a hold of that embarrassing memo.

Let's See It

There may be times when you want to print a text block. You might be worried that a certain paragraph is too catty for the company newsletter, so you print it out and have a cohort read it. Or perhaps you just want to prove to your boss that you really have been working today.

When you want to print a text block, follow these steps:

1. Highlight the block.

2. Open the File menu.

3. Select Print/Fax. The Print/Fax dialog box appears. In the Print options (upper left corner), notice that number 5, Blocked Text, is marked (see fig. 9.4). Guess why? You're printing a text block!

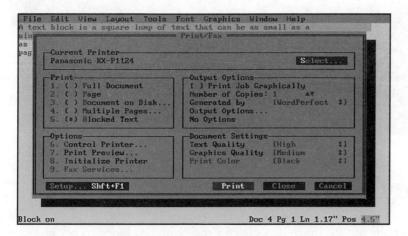

Figure 9.4
Printing blocks.

4. Set any other necessary print options.

5. Click Print or press Enter.

The text block prints just the way you want it to. Such a good, good program.

144

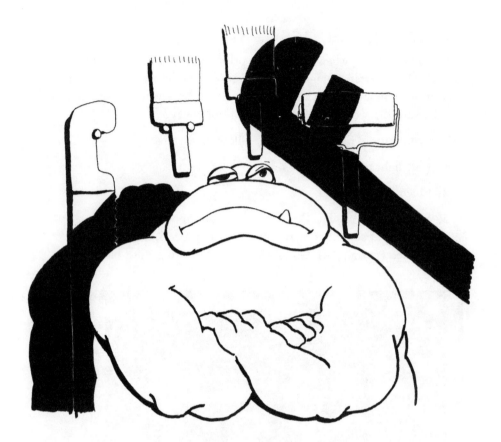

They're Out To Get Us

There's really not too much that can go wrong with text blocks. They're simple; they're friendly; and they're sugar-free. WordPerfect really knows its stuff when it comes to working with blocks of text and shouldn't give you any trouble no matter what you're attempting.

There is the human error factor, however.

It's entirely possible to highlight the wrong block. You can copy the wrong block. You can put it in the wrong place. You can accidentally delete a block you meant to keep. You can keep a block you meant to delete.

You get the idea.

If you delete a block you meant to keep, press Esc. The Undelete box appears, giving you the option of looking at your last several deletions and restoring the one you want (see fig. 9.5). Not too tough.

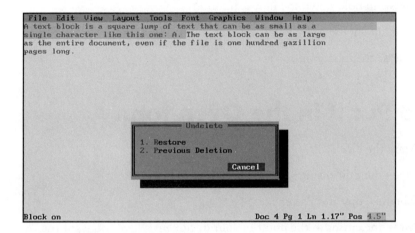

Figure 9.5
Undeleting a text block.

If you accidentally mark the wrong block, unmark it by pressing Esc.

If you copy a block to the wrong place, open the Edit menu and choose the Undo command. WordPerfect sucks that block right back up onto the invisible clipboard and waits for you to place it again.

Demon-Strations

Mark It with a B

1. Position the cursor in the paragraph you want to mark.

2. Open the Edit menu.

3. Choose the Select command.

4. Choose Paragraph.

The paragraph in which the cursor is positioned is highlighted. Good job—that block is marked forever (or at least until you press Esc).

Mark It with Another B

1. Put the mouse at the beginning of the text you want to mark.

2. Press and hold down the mouse button.

3. Drag the mouse to highlight the text you want.

4. Release the mouse button.

And Put It in the Oven for...

1. Mark the block.

2. Open the Edit menu.

3. Choose Copy and Paste.

4. Move the cursor to the point in your document where you want the copy to be placed.

5. Press Enter.

Baby and Me

1. Mark the block.

2. Open the File menu.

3. Choose Save As.

4. Type a name for the block.

5. Press Enter or click OK.

Summary

This chapter has introduced you to one of the most important concepts in WordPerfect editing: the text block. Can you build a castle? A bridge? Will you leave your Legos behind forever? The concept of text blocks is an easy one: just mark what you want to work with before you begin to work. The next encounter takes you further into the realm of editing by introducing text searches.

Exorcises

1. A text block is _____

   a. The sentence of text preceding the cursor position.

   b. Whatever you mark as a block.

   c. Thirteen words in the middle of the document.

2. Explain three ways you can mark a block of text.

3. True or false: You cannot save a single paragraph out as a file.

4. Explain how to copy a block of text.

5. True or false: Moving is not really *moving*; it's cutting and pasting text.

Oh, *There You Are!* Finding and Replacing Text

Goal

To show you a quick-and-painless editing trick that can save you from reading through that document (again).

What You Will Need

An error-ripe document and the ability to admit your mistakes.

Terms of Enfearment

search	search and replace
case-sensitive	extended search
matches	repeat searches

Briefing

You've just finished a 20-page document, the result of your research on Tasmanian wallabies. After completing the paper and preparing to submit it to the sponsoring committee, you realize with horror that you've made a rank mistake: you accidentally used the order of the species (Marsupialia) when you should have used the class (Mammalia).

They're going to laugh at you, you know.

Glancing nervously at the clock, you begin the long task of searching line by line through the bone-dry document, looking for *Marsupialia* so that you can replace it with *Mammalia.*

How much would it be worth to you to find an easier way? At least a bag of M&Ms, right?

Lost and Found

WordPerfect has something that—we admit it—just about every word processor worth its salt has: a search-and-replace feature. But this is one of the primo features of electronic text editing, one of those gotta-have-it features that make all the hassle worth it.

With search and replace (or just search), you can easily find words that you know are in there somewhere. If you're working on a single-page memo and you realize that you've misspelled your boss's name, it's one thing. But if you're working on a 100-page manuscript, getting to and fixing those errors is going to be a Big Deal.

Organizing the Search Party

WordPerfect gives you the option of choosing just a search (like when you need to find the place you talked about the dietary consideration of wallabies) or choosing a search and replace (where you find one word or phrase and replace it with another).

When you're ready to start a search, position the cursor at the point at which you want to begin the search. (In most cases, it's best to put the cursor at the beginning of the document.)

Then open the Edit menu and choose Search (see fig. 10.1). If you prefer, you can start the search by pressing F2.

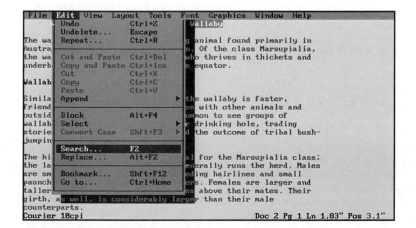

Figure 10.1
Starting out on the search.

After you select Search, the Search dialog box appears, as shown in figure 10.2.

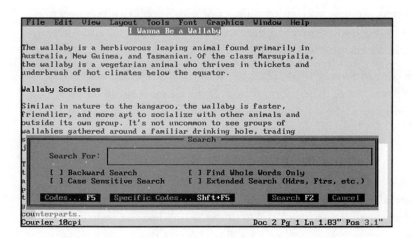

Figure 10.2
Anybody seen a class of wallabies?

In the Search For: box, type the word (or phrase) you're looking for. By the way, what are you looking for?

We're All Searching for Something

Happiness. A good pizza. Shoes that fit.

WordPerfect gives you a lot of latitude when it comes to the kinds of things you can search for. Here are the rules:

- You can search for a single word or a phrase (up to 80 characters total).

- The phrases can, of course, include spaces.

- You can search for numbers.

- You can search for a raise (but WordPerfect won't guarantee that you get one).

- You can search for codes—which are not words or numbers, but unseen codes WordPerfect uses in your document.

You type the word, phrase, or number(s) in the Search For: box. Then you can use one of the search tools to make sure that you find the something for which you're looking.

Flares and Flashlights

WordPerfect provides you with a number of search tools that you may or may not find helpful, depending on what you're searching for and where you've left the cursor. Here they are:

Backward Search. If you click in this box, WordPerfect will search backward from the cursor position. If the cursor is already at the beginning of the document (which means that you just want to be difficult), WordPerfect says in its oh-so-eloquent style

```
Not found
```

Case Sensitive Search. If you click in this box, WordPerfect will be careful of your feelings and will also search for words just the way you enter them. If you type KiDDo in the Search For box and click Case Sensitive Search, WordPerfect will find only KiDDo—not Kiddo, kiddo, or kIddO.

Find Whole Words Only. This option causes WordPerfect to find only whole words that match the Search For: text. For example, suppose that you're searching for the word

if

Why? (Oh, don't be so difficult. It's just an example.) If you don't click the Find Whole Words Only box, WordPerfect will look for anything that has those two letters in sequence. So the program will jerk to a stop every time it finds things like

thrifty

swift

rifle

ifternatius

You get the picture. It's a real hassle to find things you don't want to find. Use Find Whole Words Only anytime there's a possibility that WordPerfect will land on the wrong pad.

Extended Search. This takes the whole search idea and stretches it to include things like headers and footers, endnotes, notes, and other miscellaneous trivia.

Codes. You can click this button or press F5. WordPerfect displays a pop-up window of a trillion search codes (see fig. 10.3). You can scan through and choose the code you want to find.

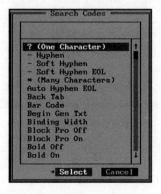

Figure 10.3
WordPerfect's answer to a decoder ring.

> WordPerfect uses special codes to control formatting, font, and other specifications in your document. You can display the document with the codes intact by opening the View menu and choosing Reveal Codes. For more about this exciting topic, see Encounter 12.

Specific Codes. Here's another one of those Look-for-me-I'm-a-code options. Press Shift+F5 or click the Specific Codes button to display the list of possible search items.

There You Are!

When you're finished packing up your search tools, you can finish the process by clicking Search or pressing F2. What happens?

Well, don't blink.

The cursor jumps to the space following the word or phrase you were searching for. Lightning fast. Concord fast.

My eyes are still rolling.

What I *Meant* To Say

Sometimes, you use the wrong word. In your memo, you said,

> We wanted to insure that this doesn't happen again.

No, no, no! Your editor crumpled it up, threw it on the floor, and jumped up and down on it. How many times does she have to tell you? It's *ensure*, not *insure!*

Okay, okay, I'll change it! You say, backing out of her office. You hurry back to your desk before security arrives. Quick—you need to replace all those insures with ensures.

Simple to do, right? Let's start with the dialog box. Press Alt+F2 (or open the Edit menu and select Replace). Figure 10.4 shows the dialog box that looms to greet you.

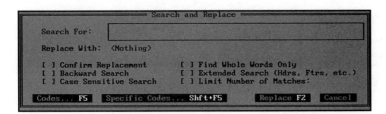

Figure 10.4
*Your mission, should
you decide to accept
it...*

Search and replace is a nice concept, don't you think? You take something away, but you make sure to plug up the hole with something else. Maybe our armed forces could use search-and-replace instead of search-and-destroy missions. Instead of searching for and destroying enemy weaponry, we could search for it, take it away, and leave something—like teddy bears—in its place.

Know What You're Looking For

To start the search and replace, you enter the word, phrase, or number you're searching for in the Search For; box (look familiar?). Then press Tab. The text-entry box moves to the Replace With: line (see fig. 10.5).

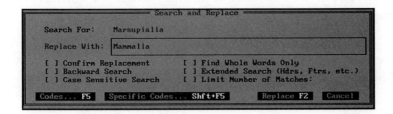

Figure 10.5
*Entering what you'll
put back.*

Proper Etiquette

The Search and Replace dialog box gives you a number of options, some similar to those in the Search box.

> **Confirm Replacement.** This is one unique to the replace experience. If you click in this box, WordPerfect will stop each time it gets to the Search word and ask you whether you want to replace the word (see fig. 10.6).

Figure 10.6

Tentative replacing: Is it okay? Are you sure?

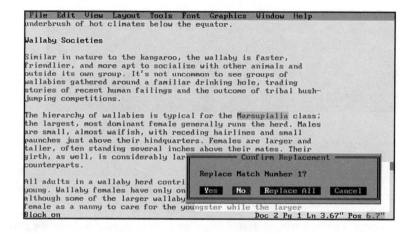

Backward Search. Remember this? You have to turn around backward at the keyboard before you use it.

Case Sensitive Search. This one, too. If this is checked, you'll cry the next time you watch Beaches.

Find Whole Words Only. Again, you saw this one in Search territory. You don't want those half-eaten words. You don't know where they've been.

Extended Search. This is the last one you discovered in the Search box. It automatically searches the pockets of your stepparents and in-laws.

Limit Number of Matches. This keeps you from using the same word too often, by limiting the number of times you can search and replace something.

Match-Making

SNPN (Single, Non-Smoking, Proper Noun) desires companionship, modification, and enhancement from SA (Single Adjective). Enjoys cursor flashing, quick formats, and late-night file retrievals.

If you're searching for something less defined (like when you can't remember—exactly—how to spell that something you're looking for). You can use certain anything-goes characters to help you locate your Something.

> You use the wildcard characters as part of the text in the Search For: box.

The anything-goes (also called *wildcard*) characters are ? and *. The question mark can stand in for any character. Only one, though. For example, if you enter the word

ma?e

You could find

make

male

made

mane

maze

And so on. The ? is replaced with any letter.

The asterisk (*), on the other hand, means "any characters." So if you enter

m*e

You would find all the words above, plus

measure

matricide

matinee

And any other word that begins with M and ends with E.

Doing It All Over Again

You searched it once. You don't want to do it again. Isn't there a quick way to repeat the search you just entered?

F2, F2.

What? What? (Is there an echo in here?)

After you've searched for something you particularly like, you can search for it again by pressing F2 and then pressing F2 again when the dialog box appears. Simple and quick.

They're Out To Get Us

You thought you were being a model student. You wanted to make your editor happy. After hearing her rant and rave about the misuse and abuse of the word *if*, you decided to do a search and replace and plug in *whether* instead. You pressed Alt+F2, entered *if* as the Search For: text, entered *whether* as the Replace With: text, and pressed F2.

Here them playing Taps in the distance? That's for you.

Because every word that had the letters i and f in it now has the letters w-h-e-t-h-e-r in i-f's place. That means that what used to be

gift

is now

> gwhethert

Hmmmm. Maybe you've created a new language, but you may not be able to communicate that to your boss.

So how do you fix it? Are you ready?

Press Ctrl+Z.

That's it. No fanfare, no hoopla. Just Undo it.

Demon-Strations

Searching in All the Right Places

1. Move the cursor to the beginning of the document.
2. Press F2.
3. Enter the text you want to search for.
4. Click whatever search options you want.
5. Click Search or press F2.

I'll Gladly Pay You Tuesday for a Hamburger Today

1. Position the cursor at the beginning of the document.
2. Open the Edit menu.
3. Select Replace (or press Alt+F2).
4. Type Search For: text.
5. Type Replace With: text.

6. Select any necessary search options.

7. Click Search or press F2.

Summary

This encounter showed you how to use one of the streamlined, rockets-on-your-fingers editing features available in WordPerfect 6.0: search and replace. You can now look for specific words, numbers, or phrases and, if you choose, replace those with other words, numbers, or phrases. WordPerfect also gives you the option of searching and replacing those mysterious hidden codes which you haven't yet learned about. (We'll get to it, don't worry.)

Exorcises

1. What's the difference between search and search and replace?

2. Which of the following options are part of the search process?

   a. Search Forward

   b. Find Whole Words Only

   c. Find Partial Words

   d. Extended Search

3. True or false: There are two different buttons for code searches, and no one really knows why.

4. With search and replace, you can _____

    a. Search for a word and replace it with another one.

    b. Replace all words without prompting.

    c. Search for your office partner and replace her with Cindy Crawford or Mel Gibson (whomever you'd prefer).

    d. Use wildcard characters.

5. 15-point bonus essay question: In 50 words or less, describe how WordPerfect's search and replace feature can enhance your life (include photos, if appropriate).

11th Encounter

How D'You Spell That?

Goal

To help you find and use WordPerfect's built-in writing tools—the speller, the thesaurus, and the grammar-checker.

What You Will Need

A pack of gold stars, a red marker, and a Milky Way candy bar.

Terms of Enfearment

speller	thesaurus
grammar-checker	correction

Briefing

WordPerfect knows that you don't like to be sitting out here alone in the land of Dangling Participles and Erroneous Spelling. And you know that a misspelling can blow your credibility—and your document—right out of the water. You've seen that look: They are reading through your report when, suddenly, they all look up at you quizzically. Carl, who was the Third Grade Spelling Champion at Saint Ignatius No. 98, says "It's s-u-p-e-r-f-l-u-o-u-s, not superfloous."

WordPerfect could have told you that.

And when you use the word *ordinarily* 14 times in the same document, that doesn't say much for your vocabulary. You couldn't have thought up even one other word that means *ordinarily*? WordPerfect can.

The biggest error is the one most people don't even catch. But accidentally put your report in front of someone who has a degree in English—or who has worked as an editor—and you're in trouble. There may be two or three words left in your document when she's through. If you're lucky. Grammar is a scary thing. That's why most of us ignore it.

WordPerfect will check your Ps and Qs for you.

Let's start with the obvious: Spelling.

Winner of the Speling Bea

When you're ready to run the spelling checker, open the Tools menu and choose Writing Tools. (Or, if you prefer, you can press Alt+F1.) Figure 11.1 shows you where the option is, just in case you've missed it.

Press Enter to select the command and another cute little pop-up box appears (see fig. 11.2). This one shows you all the writing tools available and lets you make your choice. Press 1 to choose Speller.

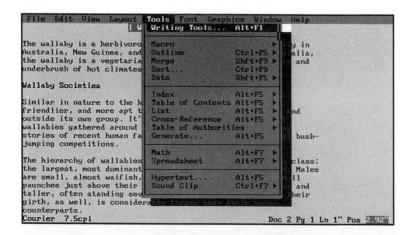

Figure 11.1
Oh writing tools, oh writing tools...

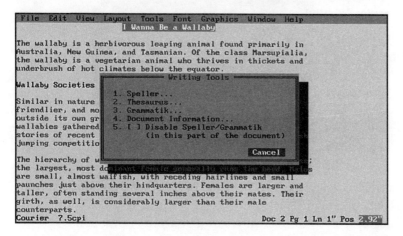

Figure 11.2
Our dessert tray...the Writing Tools menu.

Spelling Choices

Oops. Another screen. This one asks you what you want to check:

Word. Checks the word at the cursor position.

Page. Checks the current page.

Document. Checks the current document.

From cursor. Starts the spelling checker at the cursor position and goes through the end of the document.

Look Up Word. Like a search procedure, this option lets you find words that rhyme with the word you entered or that match a pattern you specify.

Edit Supplemental Dictionary. Lets you edit specialized dictionaries that you may create to use with different files.

I've Been Set Up! (Spelling)

If you're one of those people who likes to look at your salad from every

Figure 11.3
So what's to set up?

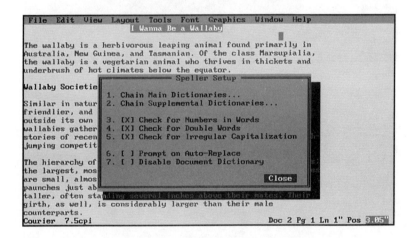

possible angle before eating it, you may want to gaze (or graze) through the Spelling Setup options. Display them by pressing Shift+F1. The Speller Setup dialog box, oh-so-conveniently shown in figure 11.3, appears.

The options that will concern you most in the Speller Setup box are probably items 3 through 5, which control what errors are found. If the speller finds any of these occurrences—numbers in words, double words words, or irRegular CaPitalization, it will alert you (and the media).

The first two—concerning dictionaries—are for the Advanced Spelling class (which doesn't meet until 2 p.m.). The last two, Prompt on Auto-Replace (which asks you before correcting errors) and Disable Document Dictionary (which takes away any custom dictionary you've added to the document), you may use every once in a while.

Obviously, to turn features on, click the little boxes to put an X in them. To turn them off, click again to remove the X. When you're finished preparing yourself, click Close.

Go, Speller, Go

Assuming that everything is set up to your satisfaction, you're ready to roll. To start the Speller, make your choice from the Speller dialog box. (Remember that? You saw it in figure 11.2.)

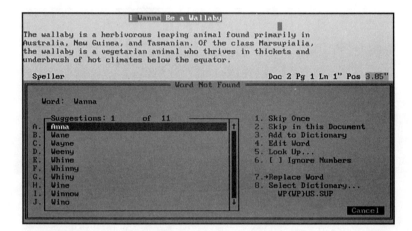

Figure 11.4
Speller in action.

WordPerfect calls its Speller into action, and, when an error is found, displays a message box with a number of possible alternative words and several options (see fig. 11.4).

The options are pretty self-explanatory: you can skip the found word this time, skip it for the whole document, add it to the dictionary, edit it, look up a similar word you specify, replace the word with one from the list, or choose a different directory.

If you want to choose a word from the list, press the letter of the word you want to use. The options you'll use most often are Skip, Add, and Replace.

When the Speller is finished, it tells you so. Click OK or press Enter.

What's Another Word for...

Do you ever get stuck in a word rut? That happens occasionally to the best of us—you subconsciously pick a word of the week and use it in everything from memos to letters to your son's teacher.

The Thesaurus can help you break the habit. Just put the cursor on the word you want to find an alternative to. (Don't highlight the word.)

Figure 11.5
What's another word for...

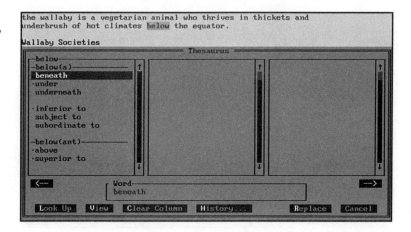

Then open the Tools menu, choose Writing Tools, and select Thesaurus. The screen in figure 11.5 meets your eager eyes.

You can find both synonyms (different word, same meaning) and antonyms (different word, opposite meaning) with the Thesaurus. Additionally, the Thesaurus provides you with several different meanings (if there *are* different meanings). You can use the following options to choose the new word:

Look Up. Allows you to look up the meaning of a word.

View. Returns to the document so that you can edit the text.

Clear Column. Removes the entries in the current column.

History. Shows the words you have looked up using the Thesaurus.

Replace. Puts the word you chose in place of the word in the document.

To choose a different word, highlight the one you want and press R (for Replace).

I Ain't Got No Harvard Larnin'

Looking for that "polished" sound? The grammar checker built into WordPerfect, called Grammatik, can do a thorough check of your document and make some far-reaching suggestions.

Start Grammatik by choosing Writing Tools from the Tools menu and then selecting option 3, Grammatik. After a moment, Grammatik appears.

> No, it doesn't? On some systems, Grammatik seems to push memory limitations to the edge. If memory is a problem for you, try exiting WordPerfect, rebooting your system, and trying again (this removes any other programs you might have had loaded). If that doesn't work, you can run Grammatik right from DOS by changing to the WPC60DOS directory (where Grammatik is stored), typing GMK, and pressing Enter.

Grammatik really deserves a book of its own, and, if you're already dealing with WordPerfect option overload, you won't be happy to see the wealth of choices you have to make in Grammatik. You can see histories of things, fine tune writing styles, compare documents, save statistics to a file and on and on...

You'll be concerned with the options in the File menu. These options allow you to choose what type of checking you want done:

- Interactive, in which the document is checked and you are asked about each error as it is found

- Resume interactive, in which you pick up after dealing with an error

■ Grammar and Mechanics, in which you check only the grammar and mechanical aspects of the file

■ Spelling only, an interactive spelling check

■ Read only, which lets you read about the errors but not correct them as they are displayed

■ Mark all errors without pausing to show user

■ Remove marks from earlier check

For our purposes, let's select Grammar and Mechanics. Grammatik goes away for a moment and then comes back with a double screen. The top screen shows your document with the suspected error highlighted. The bottom screen shows what was found and what Grammatik thinks the problem is.

In the Wallaby document, Grammatik told us

Check: Marsupialia

Advice: Spelling error.

Well, it's *not* a spelling error, so there. The program tells us that we can bypass Grammatik's well-intentioned advice by pressing F10 to go on to the next problem.

Wouldn't it be more positive if we referred to our faux pas as *learning experiences* or *challenges* instead of problems? Would Walt Disney really want us to be thinking so negatively of ourselves?

You can figure out the options at the bottom of the screen: F10 to go on, F9 to edit, F6 to ignore, F5 to ignore the word, F3 to replace it, F7 to add it to the dictionary, and F2 to replace it with something else. Pretty standard.

After everything's done, Grammatik bumps you back to the opening screen. Press T to see the statistics of your file. The most interesting stuff on this screen is the Flesch Reading Ease and Flesch-Kincaid scores: These tell you the readability of your piece. The best range, they say, is between 8th and 10th grade level (scary, huh?). Our wallaby example rated a 44 (Difficult), with a grade 12 reading level.

If you press Enter, a summary screen is displayed, telling you what each of your scores mean. Press Esc to return to the main menu.

Here's an interesting thing to do: Open the Statistics menu and choose Comparison charts. This places your file (or in this case, the Wallaby document) beside great pieces of literature like the Gettysburg address (which got a 64) and—of all things—a life insurance policy.

You can save your statistics to a file. The command you need is in the Statistics menu.

When you are ready to exit Grammatik, open the File menu and choose Quit. (And try not to take the corrections too personally.)

File Stats

Announcer: Well, we clocked that last paragraph at close to 1.4 seconds. That's quite an improvement over the last paragraph. What do you think, Jim?

Jim: Amazing, amazing. Some of the best paragraphs I've seen this season. Now, for an in-depth report, we're going down to Carl in the field. Are you there, Carl?

How's your document looking? Do you care about how many characters, words, and lines long it is, how many words you've used per sentence, how long the longest sentence is (you might have sentences that just go on and on and on, rather like this one)?

Well, in some situations, you might care. If you're entering the Writer's Digest Annual Writing contest, for example, you need to make sure that your piece isn't one word longer than 2000. If so, beeeeep! You're disqualified.

And even in more "normal" situations like trying to write a brief PR letter, trying to target an effective resume, or trying to prove wrong the person who told you "You couldn't say, 'This sky is falling' in less than a hundred words!" (apparently some kind of shot at your long-windedness), the file stats could come in handy.

To display the statistics of your document, select Writing Tools (by opening the Tools menu and choosing Writing Tools or by pressing Alt+F1). Then choose option 4, Document Information. Another screen appears, telling you the particulars of your document (see fig. 11.6).

Figure 11.6
Crucial file information you never care to see.

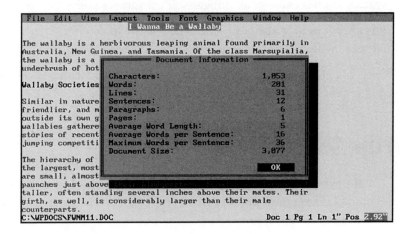

After you've looked everything over, click OK. You are returned to the document.

Well, *that* was exciting, wasn't it?

They're Out To Get Us

Sorry, I'm a Moron

What's the worst thing you can do while you're running the spelling checker? (Besides running over the cat's tail with your desk chair.)

Here's a candidate: Add misspelled words to the dictionary.

Oh, you're chugging right along. There are lots of words that are unique to your industry that WordPerfect keeps hanging up on. You've been adding words left and right by using option 3 in the Word Not Found box.

The front of your brain is thinking about what to have for lunch. That antipasto salad from Greek Tony's sounds really good, but you like those little mini pizzas from Pizza Hut, too. But Pizza Hut is farther, and you just went there day before...

What?

A little voice in the back of your brain is saying "What was that? Did you see that word? Did you just press 3 to add that word to the dictionary?"

Maybe you did, and maybe you didn't. You're not sure. But you sure are hungry.

How can you look at the dictionary to see whether you've added words that shouldn't have been added? Well, first, pay closer attention to the rest of the spelling check. Then when the spell check is over, open the Tools menu and choose Writing Tools. Then select Speller. From the next menu, choose Edit Supplemental Dictionary. Another pop-up box appears, asking you what dictionary you want to edit (see fig. 11.7). Because you are still working on the same document, choose Document Specific.

Another screen, creatively entitled the Edit Supplemental Dictionary screen, appears. Use the commands at the bottom of the window (Edit, Add, Delete, or Name Search) to get the misspelled words out of there.

Figure 11.7
Keep your eyes peeled.

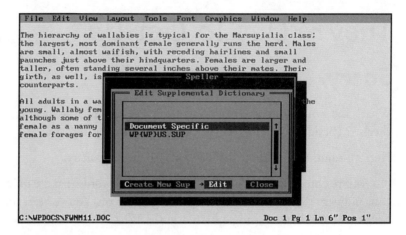

Demon-Strations

M-i-s-s-i-s-s-i-p-p-i

1. Move the cursor to the beginning of the document.

2. Open the Tools menu.

3. Choose Writing Tools.

4. Select option 1, Speller.

5. Choose Document (or any other option you want).

6. When the Word Not Found dialog box appears, select the necessary options.

Azure Flash (Blue Moon)

1. Move the cursor to the word you want to change.

2. Open the Tools menu.

3. Choose Writing Tools.

4. Select option 2, Thesaurus.

5. Use the arrow keys or the mouse to select the word you want to use.

6. Click Replace.

Summary

Feeling a little braver now? Even if you're not a writer, editor, or grammarian, WordPerfect comes chock full of tools you can use to make yourself sound as good as possible. The Speller looks for typos (and a few other things), the Thesaurus provides you with alternative word choices, and Grammatik teaches you about your own writing and helps you fix common English mistakes.

Now go get yourself that Milky Way. You deserve it.

Exorcises

1. True or false: You must always spell check the entire document.

2. Mix and Match:

      _____ Spelling Checker   a. Finds alternative words

      _____ Thesaurus   b. Checks for typos and double
                                       words

      _____ Grammatik   c. Analyzes writing strength

3. To display the Writing Tools menu, you _____.

4. True or false: You can display both synonyms and antonyms in the Thesaurus.

5. What does Grammatik do?

   a. Makes you feel bad about your writing.

   b. Evaluates your writing level and make suggestions for strengthening.

   c. Creates a report of errors.

   d. Stops at each error and shouts "Hey, you!"

   e. Threatens to call your high-school English teacher.

   f. Provides advice for best use of sentence length and word choice.

It's All a Matter of Perspective

Goal

To creatively visualize your success with WordPerfect (and learn about WordPerfect's different views).

What You Will Need

WordPerfect running (with some text displayed on the screen), some strawberry incense, and a lava lamp.

Terms of Enfearment

text mode
graphics mode
page mode
code mode

Briefing

Good evening, and thank you for coming. Come in and find a pillow—any one will do, just choose one that looks comfortable. Now, if you'll all assume the lotus position, we'll begin our Oooommmms.

There's more than one perspective to most things in life. There's his side and her side. There's before and after. There's this and that.

WordPerfect is no exception.

You can look at text. You can look at graphics. You can look at text *and* graphics. You can look at the codes only a programmer could love. By the end of this encounter, you'll be able to see your document in several new lights.

I'm in the Mode for Text

You've been looking at your document one way thus far in the book—the text way. *Text mode*, it's called. Figure 12.1 shows you the way it appears on-screen, in its monospaced font (10 points if you can remember what monospaced means) and its highlighted boldface characters.

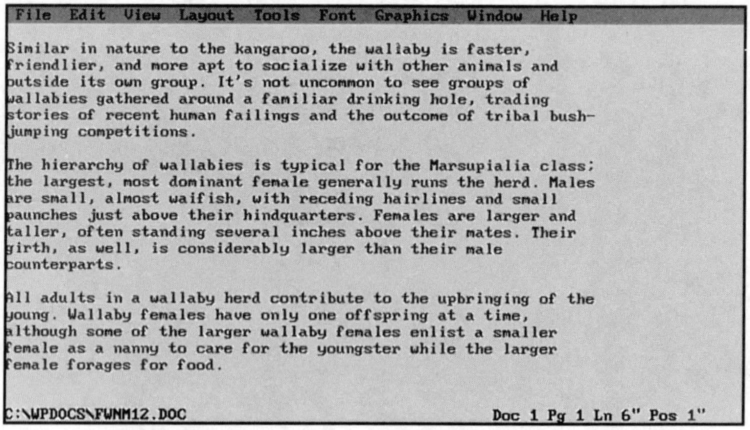

Figure 12.1
Ye ole text mode.

```
 File  Edit  View  Layout  Tools  Font  Graphics  Window  Help
Similar in nature to the kangaroo, the wallaby is faster,
friendlier, and more apt to socialize with other animals and
outside its own group. It's not uncommon to see groups of
wallabies gathered around a familiar drinking hole, trading
stories of recent human failings and the outcome of tribal bush-
jumping competitions.

The hierarchy of wallabies is typical for the Marsupialia class;
the largest, most dominant female generally runs the herd. Males
are small, almost waifish, with receding hairlines and small
paunches just above their hindquarters. Females are larger and
taller, often standing several inches above their mates. Their
girth, as well, is considerably larger than their male
counterparts.

All adults in a wallaby herd contribute to the upbringing of the
young. Wallaby females have only one offspring at a time,
although some of the larger wallaby females enlist a smaller
female as a nanny to care for the youngster while the larger
female forages for food.

C:\WPDOCS\FWNM12.DOC                          Doc 1 Pg 1 Ln 6" Pos 1"
```

We've been using the standard text mode screen—that's the way it looks when you install it. But WordPerfect offers a bunch of on-screen items that may or may not help you in your daily word processing tasks. All these items—and the other modes—are stuffed away in the View menu (see fig. 12.2).

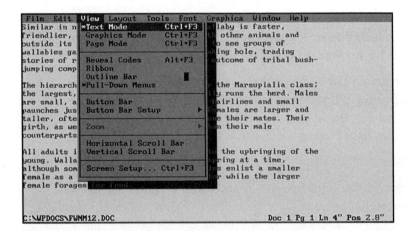

Figure 12.2
Exposing view options.

You don't need to know the ins and outs of every item you can add to the display, but we will show them to you. Figure 12.3 shows the text mode screen with all the hoopla turned on. Play around with the different items and decide for yourself which ones help and which ones simply clutter up the screen. Sometimes, less distraction means better documents.

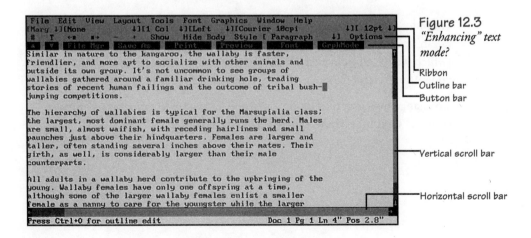

Figure 12.3
"Enhancing" text mode?

Ribbon
Outline bar
Button bar

Vertical scroll bar

Horizontal scroll bar

Good grief! That's helping? Where's the text? As a general rule, you may want to limit the "helpers" you display on the screen. For example,

- Only display the Outline Bar when you are working with the outline.

- Only use the ribbon when you are setting up your document initially (and setting the margins, text font, and size).

- The vertical scroll bar comes in handy only when you're working with documents that are longer than one or two pages, and the horizontal scroll bar may not get much use at all.

- The Button Bar gives you the same commands as those available in the File menu, so if you want to save space on-screen, you can leave the Button Bar tucked away inside the View menu. (It's nice to have those buttons right there in a convenient location, though.)

> You can customize the buttons displayed in the Button Bar by selecting Button Bar Setup (a likely option) in the View menu. This displays a pop-up menu. From this menu, you can edit the existing Button Bar, choose a different Button Bar (WordPerfect comes with six other preset Button Bars), or choose where the Button Bar is positioned.

Getting Graphics about It

Graphics mode, as you might expect, allows you to take a graphic look (that doesn't mean profanity-graphic) at your document. If you've placed art there (which we haven't covered yet and is only a nightmare on the horizon of your WordPerfect experience), you'll be able to see it in graphics mode.

To change into graphics mode, open the View menu and choose (surprise, surprise) Graphics Mode. There it is, in figure 12.4.

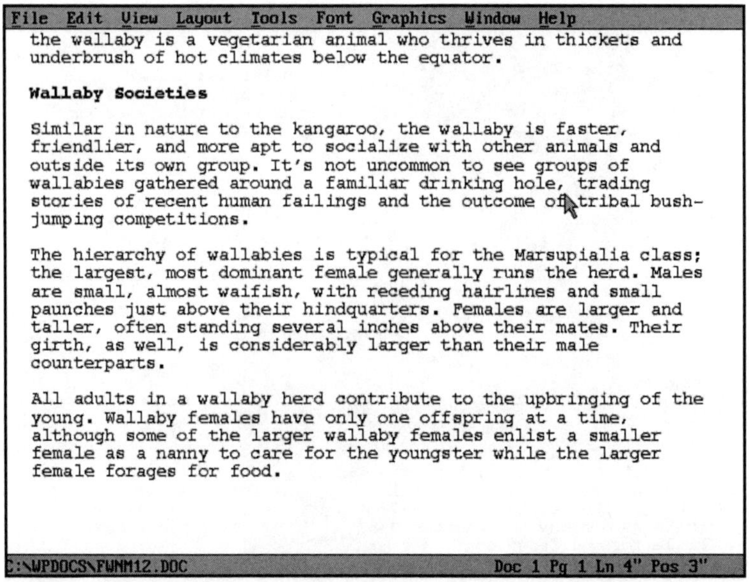

```
File  Edit  View  Layout  Tools  Font  Graphics  Window  Help
   the wallaby is a vegetarian animal who thrives in thickets and
   underbrush of hot climates below the equator.

Wallaby Societies

   Similar in nature to the kangaroo, the wallaby is faster,
   friendlier, and more apt to socialize with other animals and
   outside its own group. It's not uncommon to see groups of
   wallabies gathered around a familiar drinking hole, trading
   stories of recent human failings and the outcome of tribal bush-
   jumping competitions.

   The hierarchy of wallabies is typical for the Marsupialia class;
   the largest, most dominant female generally runs the herd. Males
   are small, almost waifish, with receding hairlines and small
   paunches just above their hindquarters. Females are larger and
   taller, often standing several inches above their mates. Their
   girth, as well, is considerably larger than their male
   counterparts.

   All adults in a wallaby herd contribute to the upbringing of the
   young. Wallaby females have only one offspring at a time,
   although some of the larger wallaby females enlist a smaller
   female as a nanny to care for the youngster while the larger
   female forages for food.



C:\WPDOCS\FWNM12.DOC                          Doc 1 Pg 1 Ln 4" Pos 3"
```

Figure 12.4
Boy, is that different.

You'll see that all the menus and commands are the same, but the text appears in a typewriter-ish style. Ugh. (That's because the text font is set to Courier, remember? If your document is set to a prettier font—say, Avant Garde—your screen will look better than this one.)

> If you had set the scroll bars and other bells and whistles on the text screen, these items will show in Graphics Mode, as well. You can remove the items—or add a few—just like you can in text mode.

What can you do in graphics mode? Everything you can do in text mode—plus one (see your graphics). You also have the luxury of zooming in on your text by using the Zoom command in the View menu. When you select Zoom, a pop-up menu of a bunch of view options appears (see fig. 12.5).

Figure 12.5

Zooming all over the place.

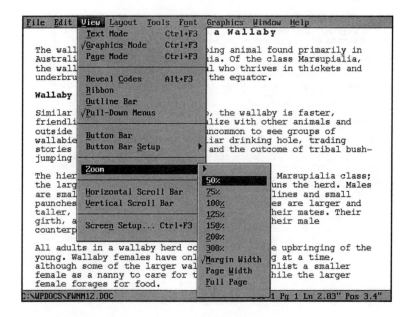

The view you see is MarginWidth. You can zoom in to 50% (which reduces the size of the document to half the screen) or up to 300% (for when your eyes are really going bad) as shown in figure 12.6.

Figure 12.6

Now, if I can just get my hearing aid fixed...

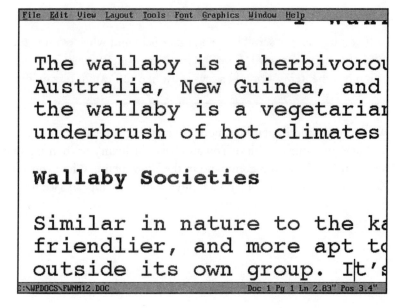

You have to say this for WordPerfect—the Graphics Mode is superior to the "graphics modes" of other popular programs. Other word processors allow you to take a look at your document in graphics mode, but they don't allow editing. WordPerfect does. Other programs get really bogged down and work like someone poured molasses in the disk drive when operating in graphics mode; WordPerfect zips right along, just as though you're working in text mode.

When you're tired of looking at that black-and-white graphics display, you can return to text mode by opening the View menu and... oh, you can figure it out.

Page a La Mode

Hmmmm. Page mode and Graphics mode? Why?

It's a subtle difference, but it's there. Page mode cannot display the smashing artwork you add to your document, but it can add something else: headers, footers, notes, etc. (Don't panic—we haven't covered those items yet.)

That's the biggest beauty of Page mode; otherwise, it looks just like Graphics mode without the pictures (see fig. 12.7).

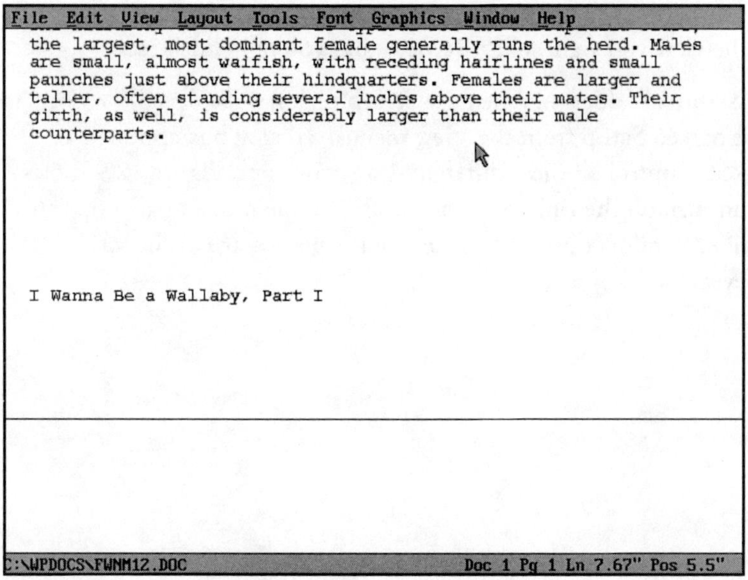
File Edit View Layout Tools Font Graphics Window Help
the largest, most dominant female generally runs the herd. Males are small, almost waifish, with receding hairlines and small paunches just above their hindquarters. Females are larger and taller, often standing several inches above their mates. Their girth, as well, is considerably larger than their male counterparts.
I Wanna Be a Wallaby, Part I
C:\WPDOCS\FWNM12.DOC
Doc 1 Pg 1 Ln 7.67" Pos 5.5"

Figure 12.7
How quaint, Henry. A footnote.

Again, in Page mode, you can edit your document, and the changes carry through to text mode when you flip back (better have somebody spot you). You have the same choices of Zoom options, so I have nothing exciting to show you there.

When you're ready to get out of Page mode, open the View menu and choose Text Mode (or another view you're interested in investigating).

The Mode Switcher

Now that you know the traditional way of choose modes, you can change easily from one view to another by pressing Ctrl+F3. A little dialog box appears in which you can choose the mode you want (see fig. 12.8).

Figure 12.8

Quick jumps to new views.

Just click the view you want, click Rewrite, and you're in business.

If you press Shift+F1 (Setup) when the Screen dialog is displayed (or when you choose Screen Setup from the View menu), a dialog box appears in which you can control all these different display options. Figure 12.9 shows that you can turn on the ribbon or Button Bar in one mode or all; you can choose various window options and control the percentage of the screen used by Reveal Codes.

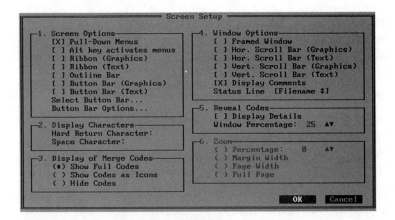

Figure 12.9
*Line 'em up and
knock 'em down.*

You've Been Framed!

The coolest thing on the Screen Setup window is an option in the Window
Options section: Framed Window. Checking this option (by clicking in it)
displays a frame around the window with a few special features (see fig.
12.10).

Close button   Title   Minimize button

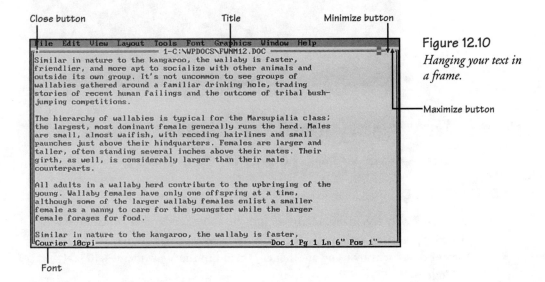

Figure 12.10
*Hanging your text in
a frame.*

Maximize button

Font

The frame gives you a few perks you didn't have before. At the top of the window, you see the file name (which use to be at the bottom). Now the default font can be displayed in the bottom left corner. In the top left corner of the frame you see a small dot. That's the *close button*. You can close the document easily by clicking on that button.

In the top right corner, you see an up-pointing and a down-pointing triangle. These are minimize and maximize buttons. When you click minimize (the down-pointing arrow), the document is reduced to thumbnail size (see fig. 12.11). This allows you to look at other documents without closing this one. When you want to return the display to normal, click the maximize button.

Figure 12.11

Al, I told you not to wash the document in hot water!

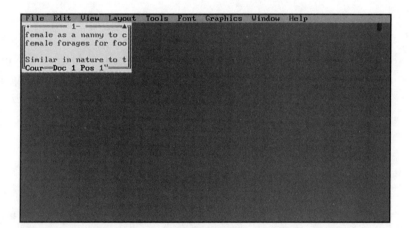

The Kangaroo Rat Hops on One Foot (Secret Codes)

Shhhh. Did the Chief give you permission to read this section?

WordPerfect has many, many behind-the-scenes codes that control the way your document looks and keeps track of itself. You can display the codes in your document by using another command in the View menu—Reveal Codes.

When you select Reveal Codes, the bottom section of the screen is turned into another window. Inside that window is the section of text at the cursor position, complete with the codes already there (see fig. 12.12).

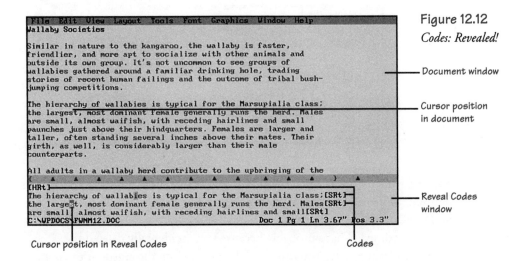

Figure 12.12

Codes: Revealed!

— Document window

— Cursor position in document

— Reveal Codes window

Cursor position in Reveal Codes

Codes

As you can see, the cursor is positioned in the document on the word *largest* in the second paragraph. In the Reveal Codes window, that same character is highlighted. In the line above the paragraph in Reveal Codes, you see the code [HRt], although nothing appears there in the regular document. That code stands for hard carriage return, which means that Enter was pressed when the cursor was positioned on that line. At the end of the line in Reveal Codes, you see [SRt], which is for soft carriage return. That's what WordPerfect puts in the text when it word-wraps your text to the next line.

Neither of these codes is too exciting. Let's cursor on up to a heading and see what's happening.

Figure 12.13 shows the cursor positioned on the first character of a heading. In Reveal Codes, you can see that the heading is boldfaced. A bold code turns on the style [Bold On], and a bold code turns off the style [Bold Off].

Figure 12.13
This isn't voyeurism, is it?

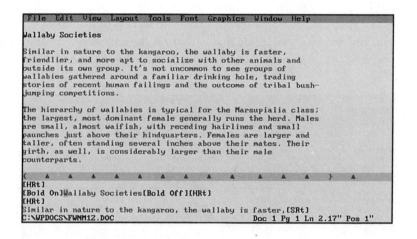

```
 File  Edit  View  Layout  Tools  Font  Graphics  Window  Help

Wallaby Societies

Similar in nature to the kangaroo, the wallaby is faster,
friendlier, and more apt to socialize with other animals and
outside its own group. It's not uncommon to see groups of
wallabies gathered around a familiar drinking hole, trading
stories of recent human failings and the outcome of tribal bush-
jumping competitions.

The hierarchy of wallabies is typical for the Marsupialia class;
the largest, most dominant female generally runs the herd. Males
are small, almost waifish, with receding hairlines and small
paunches just above their hindquarters. Females are larger and
taller, often standing several inches above their mates. Their
girth, as well, is considerably larger than their male
counterparts.
{   ▲   ▲   ▲   ▲   ▲   ▲   ▲   ▲   ▲   ▲   ▲   ▲   }   ▲
[HRt]
[Bold On]Wallaby Societies[Bold Off][HRt]
[HRt]
Similar in nature to the kangaroo, the wallaby is faster,[SRt]
C:\WPDOCS\FWNM12.DOC                    Doc 1 Pg 1 Ln 2.17" Pos 1"
```

So what will you do with these codes? If you're like most people, probably nothing, until you hit some kind of printing glitch. Perhaps you meant to underline one word and you wound up with the second half of the document underlined. That's probably because you accidentally deleted the ending underline code. You can check by positioning the cursor at the point in the document where everything went wrong and choosing Reveal Codes.

When you're tired of looking at the world in such a complicated way, open the View menu and return to text mode.

They're Out To Get Us

You'll be relieved to know that not too many things can go wrong when you're viewing WordPerfect in different modes. Possible hazards might be

- ■ **CSS.** Cluttered Screen Syndrome

- ■ **ONIOOM.** Oh-No-I'm-Out-Of-Memory! crisis

- ■ **TMV.** Too Many Views stress

- ■ **DMV.** The Department of Motor Vehicles.

Sometimes, you're so enamored with the many features of a program (after you learn to use them) that you want to gather them all around you all the time. But sooner or later, you realize that you've got a Quasimoto-like hump growing on your back; you squint constantly; and you breathe through your mouth. Unless you're growing hair on the back of your hands, don't worry—it's Cluttered Screen Syndrome. Don't make your eyes search for the words of your own document. Use only the special display tools you need. As your boss will tell you (although you might not agree); it's more important to get the job done than it is to look good while you do it.

You're sitting there, peacefully enough, playing around with different display modes. Then—dunh, da, DHUNNNNN!—ONIOOM, the Oh-No-I'm-Out-Of-Memory! crisis. WordPerfect's graphics mode demands that you have a good graphics card and at least 480K of RAM (available memory). If you get the error—boy, that's frustrating—exit the program and restart your computer to make sure that you don't have any other programs loaded, using memory you could use for graphics mode.

TMV stress is a result of all the freedoms we have today. There are so many things to choose from that we don't know what to pick. When should you use what view? When is graphics appropriate? Should you edit in page view? What will your officemate think if she looks over and sees you still using text mode? Remember that WordPerfect offered these modes because they perform specific functions: text mode is quickest for your basic text-entry and editing procedures; graphics mode shows you art and allows you to resize and move graphics; and page mode lets you see the little extras like headers, footers, and notes. The best bet—because it's fastest—for text dealings is text mode.

Nobody likes to go to the DMV. Unless you work there, and you're part of the "in" crowd, you suffer from DMV stress at least once a year, when it's time for the annual license-plate-fee robbery. Oh, and remember when you have to take those driving tests? Jeez, they're the worst. Oh, great. Now you've got *me* nervous.

Demon-Strations

A Graphic a Day

1. Open the View menu.

2. Choose Graphics Mode.

3. Add any necessary screen items (scroll bars, ribbon, outline bar, etc.).

4. Do any editing you need to do (move graphics, resize things, zoom up or out).

5. Return to text mode by pressing Ctrl+F3 or opening the View menu and selecting Text Mode.

Revealing Innermost Codes

1. Position the cursor at the point in the document where you would like to display codes.

2. Open the View menu.

3. Choose Reveal Codes.

4. Move the cursor as necessary to see other parts of the document.

5. When you're finished with Reveal Codes, open the View menu and choose Reveal Codes again (or press Alt+F3).

Summary

Well, this encounter has certainly lengthened your view of things, hasn't it? You probably see WordPerfect in a completely different way. Not just a blue program with white letters, WordPerfect gives you a number of different ways to make sure that the document is just the way you want it.

Exorcises

1. How many different views does WordPerfect offer?

2. What's the difference between graphics view and page view?

3. Give two reasons why you might use Reveal Codes.

4. What does a frame do?

   a. Keeps the text from spilling out into the monitor.

   b. Draws a nifty little box around your text that looks good in print.

   c. Lets you reduce your screen easily, which is great for working with multiple documents.

   d. Gives you a border so that you'll know when to quit typing at the end of a line.

5. What is the meaning of life? (Write in and let me know, will you?)

"Without It, We Couldn't Read!" (Justifying Text)

Goal

To help you push the text around and put it where you want it.

What You Will Need

A paragraph or two of text and nothing better to do.

Terms of Enfearment

left-justified	right-justified
centered	full-justified
ragged text	

Briefing

The way your text looks is really important—second only, in fact, to your overall message. When you're sure that you've said what you set out to say and checked for typos and grammatical errors, you'll be more concerned with where the text is placed on the page.

Typewriter flashback: Remember in the old days when you wanted to center the heading of a report you were typing? What did you do? You pressed Tab a few times, right? And then, if the last tab didn't get you close enough to the middle, you pressed the spacebar to make up the difference.

Those days are gone. Good riddance.

WordPerfect gives you several different choices for the way you arrange the text in your document. When you first fire up the program and start typing, WordPerfect assumes that you want *left-justification*, which means that the text lines up along the left edge but does not line up along the right.

> *Jargon alert:* When text doesn't line up along one edge or another, we call that text ragged (pronounced *rag-ged*) text.

You can also choose to align text along the right margin, creating what's known as *right-justified* text. Text that lines up on both ends (besides being anal-retentive) is called *full-justified* (or sometimes just *justified*) text. Text that is centered between the margins is—you're following this, right?—*centered* text.

Words to the Left of Me

For many people, left-justification, the default setting of WordPerfect, is the text alignment of choice. Your everyday memo expects to be left-justified. Reports seem, somehow, more personable with that ragged right edge.

Some people disagree, however, preferring that straight-laced look of full-justified text.

When might you want to use left-justified text?

- You're writing something you want someone to read (not that I'm biased or anything).

- You don't want a lot of unnecessary spaces between words in your document.

- You're writing a memo, letter, or report.

- Your boss tells you to.

Figure 13.1 shows the Wallaby document in its original state: left-justified.

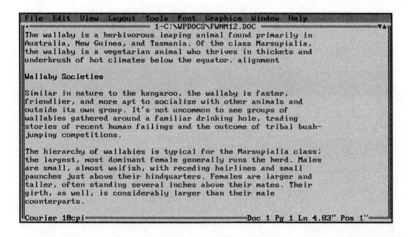

Figure 13.1

The left-justified document.

You Don't Have To Justify Yourself

Justification, or full-justification, lines the text up along both margins. The only problem with justified text is that in order to get the text justified, WordPerfect has to plug in little spaces between the words to stretch them all the way to the right margin. This looks a little contrived.

Yet, there are times when you really need to use justified text. Some of those situations might be when

- You're working with columns and you want to give the page a uniform, less cluttered look.

- You just can't stand those little ragged creatures hanging out by the right margin.

- Something inside you relaxes when your desk is straight; your pens are lined up; and your text is justified.

- Your boss tells you to.

WordPerfect gives you two different options for justifying your text. You can choose Full, which spreads just the text paragraphs to the right margin, or you can choose Full All, which spreads the heads, too. You won't be able to see the change in regular text mode; in order to see full justification, you have to go to Page mode (remember how?). Figure 13.2 shows the page in full justification, and 13.3 shows the document in Full All (strange effect, huh?).

Figure 13.2
A full job of justification.

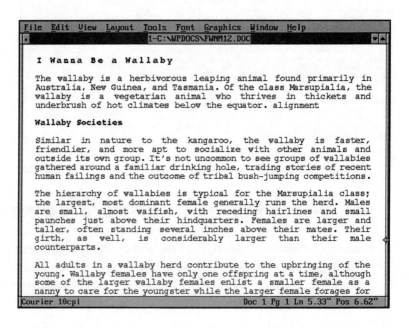

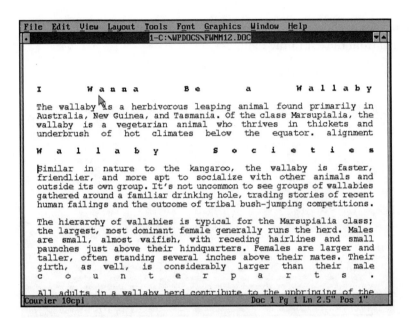

Figure 13.3
A little overboard, don't you think?

Words to the Right of Me

Aligning your text along the right margin is a dramatic effect. It makes a bold statement to the world: "I'm a non-conformist."

But you may not want to be that bold.

Take a look at the Wallaby document, shown in figure 13.4. This one is right-aligned. Having trouble thinking of times when you would want to use right-alignment? Here are a few possibilities:

- You're working on an unusual project—like advertising copy, in which the layout of the text can be nontraditional.

- You want to wake up the people in your managers' meeting.

- You want to place the text against a photo or graphic element, which will be placed on the right side of the page.

- You want to show the world how your recent political views have swung from the left to the right.

- Your boss told you to.

Figure 13.4
*Swinging to the
right.*

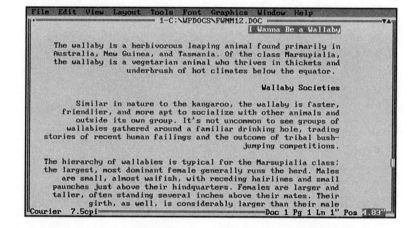

Here I Am—Stuck in the Middle with You

And then there are those among us who are the middle-of-the-road drivers, who hate to make a commitment to either side. We like our text centered and medium well, thank you very much.

Chances are, you'll use centered text sparingly, more often than not for headings and such like. Rarely, if ever, will you need to center an entire document (or large portion of text, for that matter). Reasons you might center text include

- Adding the title for your report.

- Adding the subtitle for your report.

- Adding the headings for the sections of your report (but don't you think they would look better flush left? Hint, hint, nudge, nudge.)

- You think it looks cute.

■ You're working on a stunning piece of advertising copy, rather poetic in nature, and you want to showcase your perfect prose.

■ And—everybody now—your boss told you to do it.

Figure 13.5 shows you an example of centered text. In the next section, we show you how to do all these things.

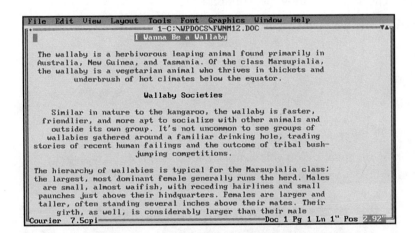

Figure 13.5
Text center stage.

Going through the Change

WordPerfect makes it easy for you to arrange the text. You can do it in two different ways:

■ You can set the way you want the text arranged throughout the whole document by using the Justification command in the Layout menu.

■ You can tell WordPerfect to change the way the text is placed in the current paragraph by choosing the Line command in the Layout menu. (You can also use the Justification command to change the current paragraph.)

Changing the Whole Shebang

Remember those mysterious codes we talked about in the last encounter? It's those codes that control how your document places text on the page. When you want to choose a different alignment, if you want the whole document to be affected, move the pointer to the beginning of the document. Then do this:

1. Open the Layout menu.

2. Choose the Justification command (click on it or press J). A small pop-up menu appears, listing these options:

   Left

   Center

   Right

   Full

   Full, All Lines

3. Choose the justification you want by clicking on it or by typing the highlighted letter (see fig. 13.6)

Figure 13.6
Choosing justification.

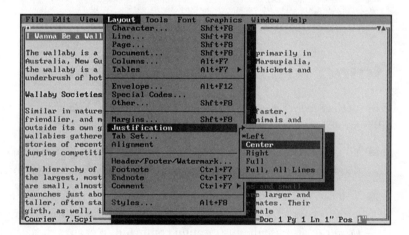

The change on-screen (unless you chose Full) is immediate. If you selected the Full or Full, All Lines, you probably have to view the document in Page or Graphics mode before you can see the full effect of the justification.

> If you want to see the code you and WordPerfect have just inserted, press Alt+F3 to reveal the codes.

Changes on a Smaller Scale

Depending on the nature of your documents, you may want to use the different justification options for different items. You might, for example, want to center the primary heading in a section by left-justifying lower headings, or you might want to center your lead paragraph but have the rest done in full justification. Whatever.

To change the justification of the current paragraph, you do the following:

1. Highlight the paragraph you want to change. (This could be a simple one-line heading, as shown in figure 13.7).

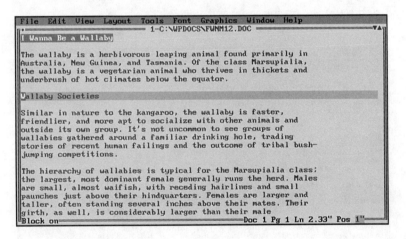

Figure 13.7
On your mark, get set...

2. Open the Layout menu and choose the Line command. The Line Format dialog box appears, as shown in figure 13.8.

3. Click the Justification style you want; then click OK.

Figure 13.8
Format!

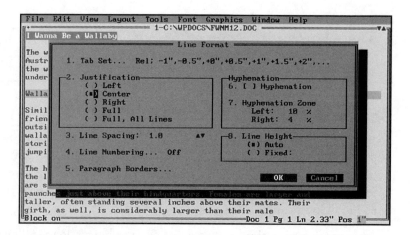

There you have it—the line is centered, as shown in figure 13.9. If you prefer, you can use the "whole document" method to change a single paragraph. Highlight what you want to change, choose the Justification command, and select the option you want.

Figure 13.9
Formatting a single paragraph.

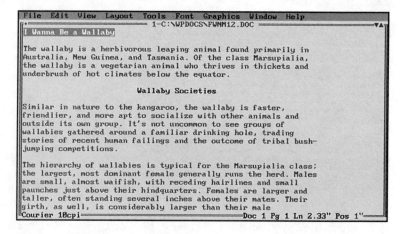

Remember styles? You can create styles that record the formatting you want and then apply it to the necessary section as needed (sort of like putting butter on a burn). Use the Styles command in the Layout menu.

They're Out To Get Us

This Looks Awful! (Doesn't it?)

Have you ever seen a four-year-old open birthday presents? He grabs one, rips the paper off, looks at the toy, puts it down. Grabs another one, rips the paper off, looks quickly at it, and puts it down. After he's gone through all of them, he says "Is there more?"

We're kind of like that, even from our vantage points of Absolute Maturity. After we learn a new trick, or several new tricks, we want to try them all. You want to center headings, left justify text, full justify text, and right-justify captions. You're mixing and matching text styles, and boy is it fun.

It's also ugly.

Fonts make that temptation even harder to fight. We can mix 10 or 20 different typefaces, alignments, and...

Hold on. Breath deeply.

Before you go sprucing up your document until it's all spruce and no trunk, remember that your primary goal is (or perhaps, should be) to communicate. Mixing text styles, alignments, and a myriad of other special effects will only overwhelm and confuse your readers. Choose one basic text style and justification and stick with it, unless you need to do something special with headings or captions or whatnot.

The urge to Go Creative is extremely strong. And you *should* cut loose, where your situation allows, but you'll produce better documents if you remember to Go Creative Sensibly.

Caffeine-Free Text

Is your text jumping around the document like it's pumped full of Maxwell House? When you try to change the format of a single paragraph, does the entire document jump to the right or the middle?

This problem could be caused by a couple of things.

Remember how WordPerfect takes care of font and formatting issues by inserting those mysterious little codes? Most things in WordPerfect are actually controlled by two codes—an On code and an Off code. When you make a word boldface, for example, WordPerfect puts a code that says "Bold on" before for the word and "Bold off" after.

The formatting commands in WordPerfect are single-shot commands. If you don't highlight the text, which tells WordPerfect where the beginning and end of the block is, WordPerfect will think you want to attach that code to the entire document—at least until you enter another format code somewhere else.

To make sure that you get the format on just the paragraph you want, highlight the paragraph first.

Demon-Strations

Justifying Your Document

1. Move the text pointer to the beginning of the document.

2. Open the Layout menu.

3. Choose Justification.

4. From the pop-up box, choose the type of justification you want.

Justifying a Line or Two

1. Highlight the area you want to change.

2. Open the Layout menu.

3. Choose Line.

4. Click the Justification setting you want.

5. Click OK.

Summary

The way you choose to align the text in your document may be a personal-preference issue, or it may be a mandate set down from higher-ups. No matter who's responsible for the decision, WordPerfect makes it easy for you to position your text pretty much any way you want it. You can choose from left-justified, right-justified, full-justified, and centered text. The next encounter follows up on the formatting theme by showing you how to work with margins and page features.

Exorcises

1. Mix and match:

    _____ Centered   a. Aligns along left margin

    _____ Full   b. Aligns along right margin

    _____ Left   c. Aligns to both margins

    _____ Right   d. Aligns in center

2. What does Full, All Lines do?

3. When might you use full-justified text?

4. Which of the justification styles is used most often?

5. For best results, _____

   a. Use full-justification in your documents.

   b. Center memos.

   c. Use at least three different types of alignment in each document.

   d. Before you swim, wait at least 30 minutes after eating.

   e. Use one basic justification style with a secondary style for headings.

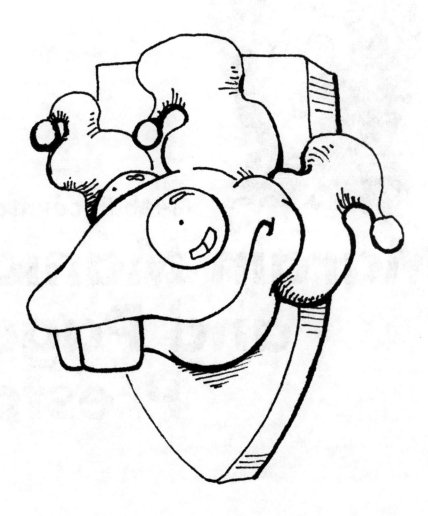

14th Encounter

Margin Mania and Page Presto

Goal

To cover all those annoying but necessary (and one or two unnecessary) things that you'll have to face sooner or later.

What You Will Need

Dry twigs, a can of Beanie Weanies, and four Twinkies.

Terms of Enfearment

margins   indents
hanging indents   page breaks
columns

Briefing

We're getting right down to the wire here. This encounter covers some of the last few basics you need in order to squelch those WordPerfect fears once and for all. You've heard of margins, right? (Not the little green men from Outer Space the FBI won't tell us about). In this encounter, you learn to put 'em in, take 'em out, and move 'em all around. There are also some page items we need to cover—things that don't fit neatly anywhere else. Things like page breaks and columns and jumping around in the document (two, three).

All of that, jam-packed into this encounter.

Lucky you.

My Favorite Margins

The word *margin* is the technical term for the white space that surrounds your text. You can't type there. You can't print there. The margins are there to protect your text just in case you drop the page on the floor, kind of like a little pillow-action.

Your page has four margins, one on each edge of the page. These margins are named for the edge they occupy: top, left, right, and bottom.

WordPerfect lets you change the space used for each of those margins. You can move things way in, like setting a 3-inch left margin (but why?), or you can move things way out (but best advice is to not set margins any smaller than WordPerfect's preset 1-inch).

Setting margins is a simple business. (Hear the 50s sitcom music in the background?):

1. Open the Layout menu.

2. Choose Margins (press M or click on the command).

The Margin Format dialog box appears, as shown in figure 14.1. So far, so good.

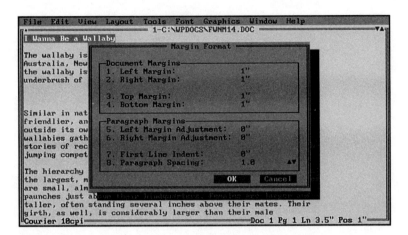

Figure 14.1
Enjoying yourself? Marginally.

There you find yourself presented with a choice right off the bat. Do you want to set Document Margins—for the whole document—or Paragraph Margins? What you do next depends on your answer to that question:

■ If you want to change the margins for a page or more, choose Document Margins.

■ If you want to change the margins for a few paragraphs (like for an indented quote), select Paragraph Margins.

> If you want to change the margin for a few paragraphs, highlight the text you want to change before you open the Layout menu and select the Margins command.

Doing the Document

To change the margins of the entire document, first position the cursor at the beginning of the document. Then open the Layout menu, choose Margins, and press 1 to choose Left Margin. A rectangle surrounds the left margin value. Type 2.5 and press Enter twice. The dialog box disappears, and the text is instantly moved inward on the screen (see fig. 14.2).

Figure 14.2
Changing the
document margins.

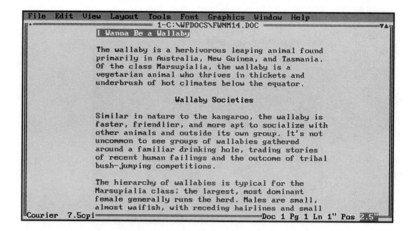

Picking a Pair of Paragraphs

There will be times when you want to indent (or outdent) selected paragraphs. Remember those awful research papers in high school in which you had to have a certain number of quotes, a certain number of footnotes, and a certain number of resources? Those quote paragraphs—called block quotes —had to be indented from both the right and left margins.

The first step in indenting selected text is to highlight the text you want to use. Mark the text as a block; then open the Layout menu and choose Margins. Finally, select Left Margin Adjustment. A rectangle highlights the value.

Remember that any value you enter will be added to the Left Margin amount in the Document Margins. As figure 14.3 shows, the left margin of the Wallaby document is already 2.5; now, by adding .25 as the Left Margin Adjustment, we bring the Total Left Margin to a whopping 2.75 inches.

Indent, Indent, Indent!

Some teachers are real sticklers for that paragraph-opening indent. In fifth grade, I asked my teacher "How big should the indent be?" after she put a big red O at the beginning of all the paragraphs in my book report. (I never did find out why she scribbled an O for *indent*.)

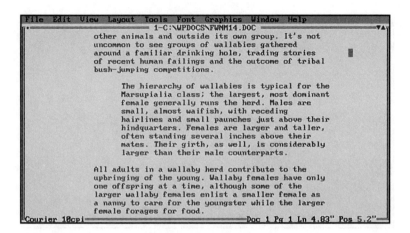

Figure 14.3
Adding a paragraph left margin on top of the document margin.

She peered at me over the top of her pince-nez glasses. "About as wide as your thumb."

I held up my thumb and looked at it thoughtfully. Then I held up my other thumb. "My left thumb seems to be smaller than my right," I said. "Which thumb would you prefer?"

I never did get that indent thing straight. I was still switching off thumbs until word processing came along.

WordPerfect lets you set a perfectly accurate indention for your paragraph openings. The First Line Indent, in the Margin Format box, does the trick. Just press 7 to select that option and type the value you want (in inches).

You'll never have to look at your thumbs again.

Spacey Paragraphs

Another option in the Margin Format dialog box lets you control the amount of space after your paragraphs. The regular setting is one line, but you can increase that (by clicking on that cute little up-pointing triangle).

Each time you click, the Paragraph Spacing value is raised by .10. If you want to reduce the space following the paragraph, click the down-pointing arrow. You can go all the way to zero.

Figure 14.4 shows a Paragraph Spacing setting of 1.5.

Figure 14.4

The roomy back-end of the sample paragraph.

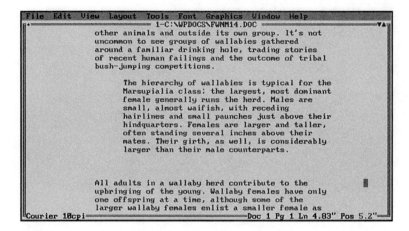

Pages

As your documents get longer and longer, you'll start to worry about Page Stuff. You've got only three paragraphs on this first page, but you really want to start a new section after that point. How do you make WordPerfect move the rest of the text to the next page? And then how to do you get to the other pages after you get the text there? Finally, can any sane person put text in columns or is that a feat better left to daredevils?

Breaking Pages

It's a familiar story: The two paragraphs have been together since their creation. Because of Paragraph Spacing and a few other saucy options, they've grown apart.

They need to break away.

When you want to give your paragraphs a helping hand and insert that page break, it's a simple task. Position the cursor at the point in your document after which you want the page break to be added.

Then press Ctrl+Enter. A double-line appears at the cursor position, and the cursor moves down to the next line (see fig. 14.5).

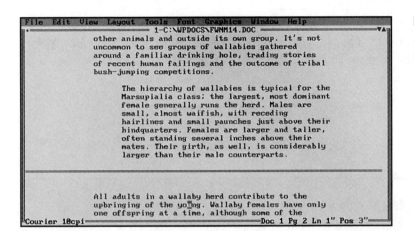

Figure 14.5
Breaking up isn't hard to do.

You can also make WordPerfect print a certain page on a certain page. For example, suppose that it's real important that WordPerfect print page 3 on a left-hand page. You can do that using the Force Page options in the Page Format dialog box (which you display by opening the Layout menu and choosing Page).

If you want to delete a page break (is reconciliation on the horizon?), just press the backspace key until the line disappears.

Use the Styles command on the Layout menu to record the settings of paragraph formats you use often.

Moving to Different Pages

Suppose that you've been typing happily away for hours and that you've created pages and pages and pages of text. How do you get back to page 2? Easy.

Open the Edit menu and drag the pointer all the way down to the last option, Go to. This displays the Go to box shown in figure 14.6. Just type the number of the page you want to see and press Enter. Then—zap!—you're there.

Figure 14.6
Are you flying first class or coach?

> WordPerfect has a feature known as bookmarks that help you insert little tags in the document at places you need to return to easily. You can create bookmarks by using the Bookmark command in the Edit menu.

Creating Columns

When you want to create a columnar effect (Hail, Caesar!) in your documents, use the Columns command in the Layout menu. This displayed the Text Columns dialog box, which gives you a couple of options (see fig. 14.7).

The easy way out is to let WordPerfect set the width and style of your columns for you—at least the first time or two you attempt this column thing.

There are four different types of columns you can choose:

➤ ■ **Newspaper columns.** With these guys, the text runs down the page, hits the bottom, and starts back up at the top.

■ **Balanced newspaper.** These columns are the same as the standard newspaper, except that WordPerfect makes sure that they are the same length.

■ **Parallel columns.** In these columns, the text is aligned so that the next item in the left column doesn't begin until the last item in the right column finished. This is good for two column tables.

■ **Parallel columns with block sunscreen protector.** This keeps your columns from suffering from ultraviolet rays and keeps them together on a page.

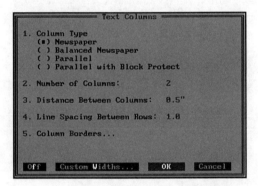

Figure 14.7
Options for building columns.

Next, enter the number of columns you want on the page. (WordPerfect will limit you to 24 columns, which is so ridiculous it's not worth talking about.) To change the number of columns, press two to select Number of Columns. Then type the number of columns you want.

You can change the spacing between the columns or the line spacing between the rows, but why mess with perfection?

Lastly, select Column Borders if you want to add a nifty neat-o border around the perimeter of your text columns.

Click OK or press Enter, and you've got columns (see fig. 14.8).

Figure 14.8
In the blink of an eye—columns.

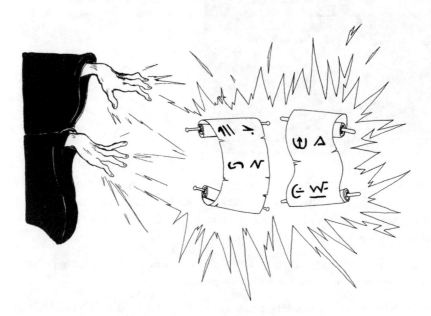

File Edit View Layout Tools Font Graphics Window Help

All adults in a wallaby herd contribute to the upbringing of the young. Wallaby females have only one offspring at a time, although some of the larger wallaby females enlist a smaller female as a nanny to care for the youngster while the larger female forages for food.

Similar in nature to the kangaroo, the wallaby is faster, friendlier, and more apt to socialize with other animals and outside its own group. It's not uncommon to see groups of wallabies gathered around a familiar drinking hole, trading stories of recent human failings and the outcome of tribal bush-jumping competitions.

hairlines and small paunches just above their hindquarters. Females are larger and taller, often standing several inches above their mates. Their girth, as well, is considerably larger than their male counterparts.

Similar in nature to the kangaroo, the wallaby is faster, friendlier, and more apt to socialize with other animals and outside its own group. It's not uncommon to see groups of wallabies gathered around a familiar drinking hole, trading stories of recent human failings and the outcome of tribal bush-jumping competitions.

The hierarchy of wallabies is typical for the Marsupialia

C:\WPDOCS\FWNM14.DOC   Col 2 Doc 1 Pg 1 Ln 6.33" Pos 4.3"

They're Out To Get Us

My Margins Are a Mess

What can go wrong with such things as margins, page breaks, and columns? Nothing truly major, certainly.

Maybe you've messed with your margins so much that everything is all moved around, and you're sick of it. You don't like them now any better than you did when you started, and yet you can remember what the default values are, so you can't even start over. Well, here are the defaults (one less thing to gripe about):

Document Margins
    Left Margin: 1"
    Right Margin: 1"
    Top Margin: 1"
    Bottom Margin: 1" (seeing a pattern, here?)

Paragraph Margins
    Left Margin Adjustment: 0"
    Right Margin Adjustment: 0"
    First Line Indent: 0"
    Paragraph Spacing: 1.0

Ugly Columns

Whoa... hold on there. You went through the motions of setting up columns just the way the book told you to. But you pressed Enter, eager to see the screen divide itself up and align, and now you're really sorry.

How do you get your single-column document back again?

Position the cursor at the point in your document where the columns begin. Then press Alt+F3. Remember what that does? It opens the small screen at the bottom where you can see the codes WordPerfect uses to control font and format. Notice, in figure 14.9, that the code

```
[Col Def]
```

is inserted at the beginning of the line where the columns start. (That's short for Column Definition).

To change your document from columns back to regular text, press the backspace key once and delete that code. Your document realigns itself immediately.

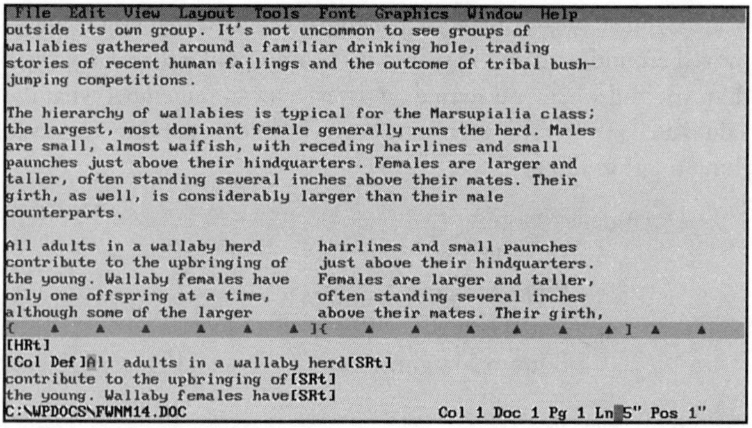

Figure 14.9
Removing unwanted columns.

```
 File  Edit  View  Layout  Tools  Font  Graphics  Window  Help
outside its own group. It's not uncommon to see groups of
wallabies gathered around a familiar drinking hole, trading
stories of recent human failings and the outcome of tribal bush-
jumping competitions.

The hierarchy of wallabies is typical for the Marsupialia class;
the largest, most dominant female generally runs the herd. Males
are small, almost waifish, with receding hairlines and small
paunches just above their hindquarters. Females are larger and
taller, often standing several inches above their mates. Their
girth, as well, is considerably larger than their male
counterparts.

All adults in a wallaby herd        hairlines and small paunches
contribute to the upbringing of     just above their hindquarters.
the young. Wallaby females have     Females are larger and taller,
only one offspring at a time,       often standing several inches
although some of the larger         above their mates. Their girth,
{    ▲    ▲    ▲    ▲    ▲ ▲ }{  ▲    ▲    ▲    ▲    ▲ ▲ ] ▲   ▲
[HRt]
[Col Def]All adults in a wallaby herd[SRt]
contribute to the upbringing of[SRt]
the young. Wallaby females have[SRt]
C:\WPDOCS\FWNM14.DOC                   Col 1 Doc 1 Pg 1 Ln 5" Pos 1"
```

Demon-Strations

A Margin for Your Thoughts

1. Move the cursor to the point where you want to change the margin. If you want to change a few paragraphs, highlight the text you want to change.

2. Open the Layout menu.

3. Choose Margins.

4. If you want to set the margin for the entire document, select the Document Margins setting you want to change and enter a new value.

5. If you want to set the margin for selected text, use the Paragraph Margins options.

6. Click OK or press Enter.

A Good Page Break Is Worth a Thousand Words

1. Position the cursor at the point after which you want the page break added.
2. Press Ctrl+Enter.

Columnizing

1. Position the cursor where you want the columns to begin.
2. Open the Layout menu.
3. Choose Columns.
4. Select the column type.
5. Specify the number of columns.
6. Change any other necessary settings.
7. Click OK or press Enter.

Summary

This encounter has provided a three-pronged approach to finishing off the details of document basics. You've learned to set and modify document and paragraph margins, insert and delete page breaks, move to different pages, and create columns. The next encounter starts Part Four by showing you how to add some important little extras to your WordPerfect documents.

Exorcises

1. The first step in setting paragraph margins is _____

   a. Opening the Layout menu.

   b. Pressing Shift+F8

   c. Highlighting text

2. True or false: Paragraph margins override document margins.

3. What two other paragraph options can be set in the Paragraph Margins settings?

4. Explain the two steps involved in setting a page break.

5. Put the following in order:

   _____ Specify the number of columns.

   _____ Click OK or press Enter.

   _____ Position the cursor.

   _____ Choose Columns.

   _____ Open the Layout menu.

   _____ Set other options.

Headsies, Feetsies, and Other Miscellaneous Bits

Goal

To inspire you into adding those extra-special some-things that help your documents look like you know what you're talking about.

What You Will Need

Some amount of text that will qualify as a document and some time to play.

Terms of Enfearment

header	footer
footnote	endnote
comment	watermark

Briefing

Unless you've been instructed to do so, adding headers, footers, and other miscellany is an optional issue. Most of us shy away from it. Why, you ask? It just *sounds* complicated, like something better left to the WordPerfect Wizards. Something else you don't need to stress about.

In the early days of word processing, adding headers and footers was a big deal. You had to know the codes. You had to get the spacing right. You had to help the program calculate how much room to leave between the edge of the page and the beginning of the text.

Just thinking about it can give you hives.

In today's WordPerfect, the process is so automated that you'll never break out in a sweat. A couple of commands, a few words, and you're in business.

Discovering Document Poles: Headers and Footers

At the far north end of the document page, above the first line of text, we have a blank space where a header could be. What *is* a header? A line of text that contains information that you want printed at the top of every page (or on alternating pages) in your document.

> You can add two headers—Header A and Header B—and two footers—Footer A and Footer B in the document. You can enter different headers and footers on each page.

Not all documents need headers. Think about what your particular document might need up there, to help readers remember what they're reading and who wrote it. You might include things like:

- The name of the book you're writing
- Your department name

- The fact that you're due for a raise
- Your company's name
- The date
- The chapter title
- The page number
- The section title

A footer is text at the bottom of your document, providing the same basic information. People come up with all kinds of things for headers and footers. For example

      I Wanna Be a Wallaby   Page 3

could be the header, and

      Murray   December, 1993

might be the footer.

Experiment. You'll get the idea,

Heads I Win

When you're ready to add a header to your document, just open the Layout menu and choose Header/Footer/Watermark. The dialog box shown in figure 15.1 appears.

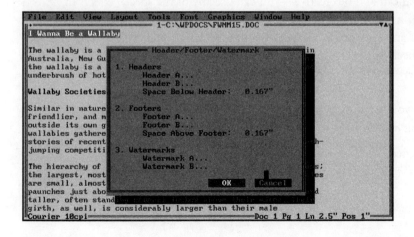

Figure 15.1
Head and feet of waterfowl dialog box.

To add the header, click on Header A (or press 1). The name is highlighted. Press Enter. Another teeny box appears, asking whether you want to add this planned header to all pages in your document, just even pages, or just odd pages. (If the documents you write are like mine, *all* the pages are odd.) Make your selection and click Create (see fig. 15.2).

Figure 15.2
All, even, or odd—
you're it!

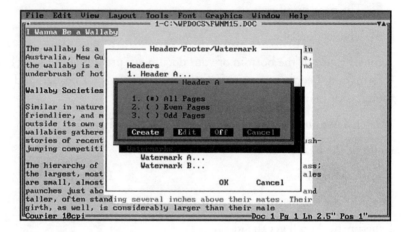

After you click Create (or press Enter—Create is highlighted), a full-sized blank screen appears. Don't panic; your document didn't go anywhere. This is the header screen. Type your header as you would any text (see fig. 15.3).

> Go ahead and be creative—you can use any of the special effects in your headers and footers that you use in your document. Change the font and size, make the thing boldface or italic, whatever. Knock yourself out.

When you're finished, press F7. The display flips back to the document, and nothing *appears* to have changed.

Stay tuned...

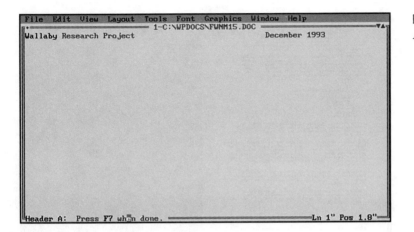

Figure 15.3
Heads up.

Tails You Lose

Adding a footer south of the border is no harder than anything else. Again, open the Layout menu and choose Header/Footer/Watermark. The same dialog box appears. Press 2 to select Footer A. Click OK or press Enter.

Same screen, right? Type your text, add any styles you want, and press F7. WordPerfect returns you to your document. Things look the same, right?

> What the heck's a watermark? A watermark allows you to add text or art *behind* document text. Select a watermark as you would a header or footer, and when the watermark screen appears, type the text or place the image (use the Graphic menu's Retrieve Image command) in the screen. When you're finished, press F7.

There They Are!

If you want to see the header and footer and make sure that you really did enter them, change to Page mode by opening the View menu and choosing Page Mode. There they are—right where you left them (see fig. 15.4).

Figure 15.4

Displaying headers and footers.

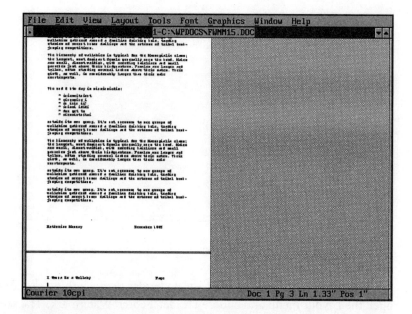

To edit the header or footer you've added, open the Layout menu, choose Header/Footer/Watermark, click the header or footer you want to edit, click OK, and select the Edit button. When the item is displayed on the screen, edit it as you would any other text and press F7 when you're done.

But I Just Want a Page Number!

Here's one of those things you expect to be easy but turns out to be difficult. Some things in WordPerfect are easier than they look; adding page numbers in headers is harder. In fact, if you're really set on adding a page number where a header or footer should be, consider changing the header or footer into a page number.

Huh?

Really, it's easier. When you want to set a page number, open the Layout menu and choose Page. The Page Format dialog box appears. Click 1, Page Numbering. The Page Numbering dialog box appears, as shown in figure 15.5.

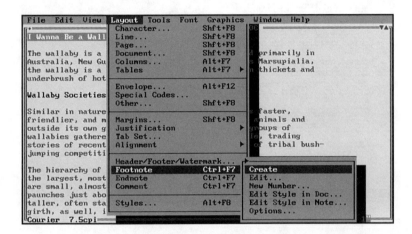

Figure 15.5
Putting in a page number.

Select option 6, Page Number Format. A rectangle surrounds the text-entry area. Type your information like this:

Wallaby Research Project, [page #]

Click OK or press Enter. You return to the Page Numbering screen.

Now, choose option 1, Page Numbering Position. The Page Number Position dialog box appears, showing you the different areas you can place the number (see fig. 15.6). If you want to use the number as a header, click one of the Top options. If you want to use the number as a footer, click one of the Bottom options. Then click OK.

Figure 15.6

The Page Number Position box.

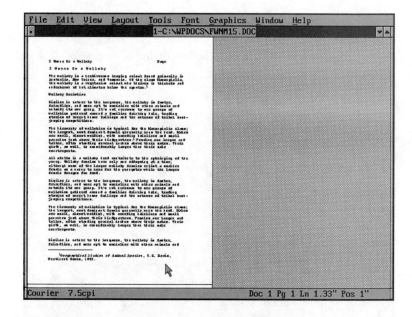

Pretty big hassle, huh? And this is the easy part!

When you're ready to see how it looks, open the View menu and choose Page Mode. As you can see in figure 15.7, two items appear in the header line: Header A, which says "I Wanna Be a Wallaby" and the page number, which was set to read "Wallaby Research Project, [page #]".

Dr. Scholl's Footnotes

Aren't you impressed with yourself when you have an excuse to use footnotes? They look so—scholarly. With WordPerfect, adding, keeping track of, and printing footnotes is a snap. Here's how:

1. Position the cursor at the point you want to add the footnote.

2. Open the Layout menu.

3. Choose Footnote. A small pop-up box appears, giving you several additional options (see fig. 15.8).

4. Select Create. The Footnote screen appears. A 1 is already entered on the screen if this is your first footnote.

5. Type your text and press F7. The footnote is added.

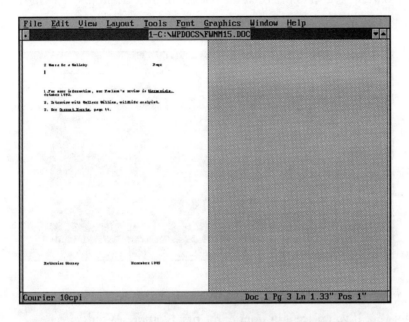

Figure 15.7
Finally, a page number.

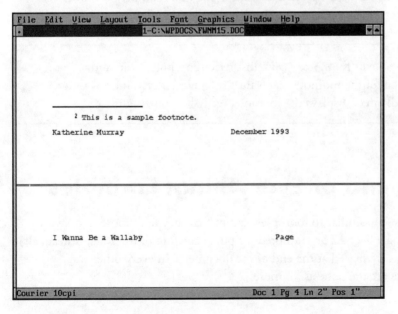

Figure 15.8
Footnote possibilities.

Again, in order to see the footnote in your document, you have to use Page mode. A footnote is always placed at the bottom of the current page (see fig. 15.9).

Figure 15.9
Aren't we smart?

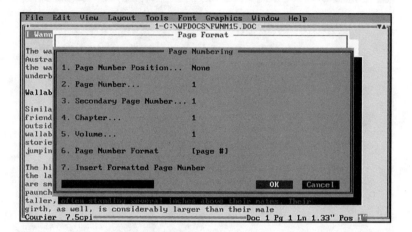

If you add another footnote on the page, WordPerfect automatically numbers it for you. If you place it in front of the first footnote, WordPerfect renumbers the other footnotes so that they are in order.

You can edit footnotes easily. Just select Footnote, Edit, and type the number of the footnote you want to change. After you press Enter, WordPerfect displays the footnote, ready for you to edit.

The End of Everything: Endnotes

Endnotes are similar to footnotes, except that they have more to do with "end" than "feet." The endnote isn't put at the foot of the page; instead, all the notes are placed at the end of the document. In every other way, endnotes are the same as footnotes.

When you want to enter an endnote, first position the cursor at the point you want WordPerfect to enter the number. Next, open the Layout menu, select Endnote, and choose Create. Type the endnote and press F7. Like a footnote, WordPerfect adds the note to the document (you can see the endnote number, but not the note itself). To see the note, display the document in Page Mode and go to the end of the document (see fig. 15.10).

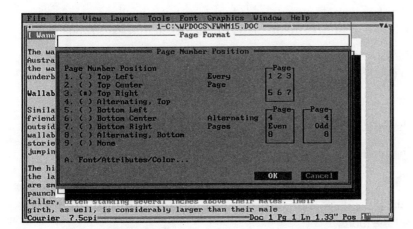

Figure 15.10
Endnotes appear at the end of the document.

They're Out To Get Us

It's possible to go a little crazy with all the notes you can add in your document. There are headers, footers, footnotes, endnotes, and comments.

Remember to use these items sparingly and to resist the temptation to assault your audience with a barrage of information—however useful it might seem to you.

When Is a Footnote an Endnote?

You've finished your document, added the footer, put in all the notes, and you're ready to print, you think. Better take a look at it in Page Mode first.

What does Page Mode reveal? A footnote above the footer at the bottom of the page (see fig. 15.11).

Whether or not you can allow this will depend on three things:

- The amount of text in your footnote.
- The amount of text in your footer.
- Whether you can instead use the footnote as an endnote.

If possible, make the footnote and endnote, or, if necessary, suppress the display of the footer.

Figure 15.11
Conflicting feet.

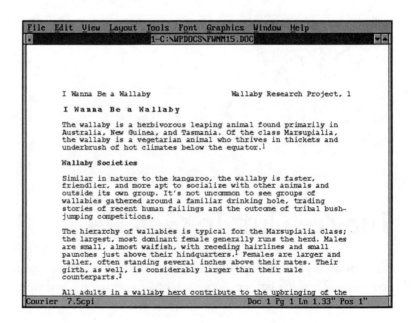

Demon-Strations

Put a Head on That, Will Ya?

1. Open the Layout menu.

2. Choose Headers/Footers/Watermark.

3. Select Header A.

4. Click OK.

5. Choose where you want the header to appear (All Pages, Even Pages, or Odd Pages); click Create.

6. Type the header and add any necessary styles.

7. Press F7.

A Footnote by Any Other Name

1. Position the cursor at the point where you want to add the footnote number.

2. Open the Layout menu.

3. Choose Footnote.

4. From the pop-up menu, select Create.

5. On the Footnote screen, type the footnote you want to add. (WordPerfect adds the number for you.)

6. Press F7.

If you want to see what the footnote looks like, open the View menu and choose Page Mode.

Summary

This encounter enables you to add the finishing touches to your document. Headers, footers, footnotes, and endnotes can help you provide your reader with information about the document you've created. The next encounter looks at yet another high-end feature that gives most of us the heebie-jeebies: adding art.

Exorcises

1. What's the difference between a header and a footer?

2. What's the difference between a footer and a footnote?

3. What's the point of asking all these questions?

4. Does anybody know all the words to the Carol Burnette theme song?

5. Name four items you might want to include in a header.

16th Encounter

Getting to the Art of the Matter

Goal

To help you face the epitome of word processing terror:
Graphics Dread.

What You Will Need

Some reason to learn how to incorporate graphics,
nerves of steel, and the ability to leap small doghouses.

Terms of Enfearment

graphics box   clip art

figure box   table box

text box   user box

equation box   button box

Briefing

Adding graphics is the task most people love to hate about WordPerfect. But when it comes right down to it, the process just isn't that difficult. WordPerfect lets you add art two different ways:

- You can plug the art right into the document.
- You can create a box to hold the art you add.

You also can add lines and borders and fill the graphics boxes you create with shading. Let's start with the easy stuff first.

> WordPerfect comes with approximately 30 pieces of art that you can use in your own documents, so if you don't have something of your own to play with, you can use a WordPerfect clip art file.

Ready-To-Go Graphics

When you want to put a piece of art in your document without first creating a graphics box, open the Graphics menu and choose Retrieve Image. The Retrieve Image File dialog box appears, as shown in figure 16.1. If you know the name of the art file you want to use, type it in the Filename: box. If you don't know the name or location of the file, you can use the File List or QuickList to find it.

> WordPerfect's clip art files are stored in the C:\WP60\GRAPHICS subdirectory. To display this path, press F5 and Enter; then select the file you want from the File List.

After you select the file and click OK or press Enter, WordPerfect pulls the art into your document, moving the text over. The graphics aren't placed exactly at the cursor position, but it's close enough to be warm (see fig. 16.2).

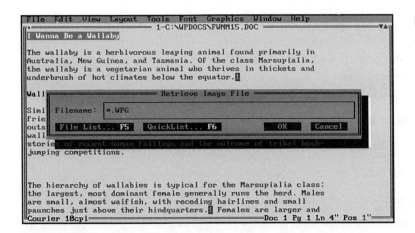

Figure 16.1
Finding the art.

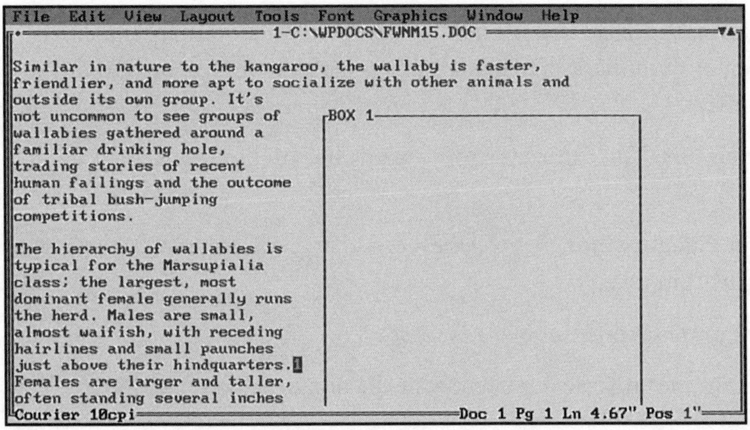

Figure 16.2
Box or art?

If you don't see an image in the box, try switching over to Graphics Mode. If the image still isn't there, don't panic—your monitor may not have enough memory to display the graphic on the screen. Try printing the document, and then, if it's not there, go ahead and panic.

Art in a Box

The other method of adding graphics involves first creating a graphics box. WordPerfect actually allows you to create eight different kinds of graphics boxes, each of which is designed to hold a specific type of art:

- **Figure box.** Stores clip art, drawings, and charts.

- **Text box.** Contains quotes, sidebars, and margin notes.

- **User box.** A borderless box that stores art images.

- **Table box.** Holds tabular information, spreadsheets, or text.

- **Equation box.** A borderless box that allows you to display equations in correct form.

- **Watermark Image box.** Remember the watermark on high-quality paper? A watermark image box places graphics (or text) behind document text.

- **Button box.** You can use art or text in a button box, which acts as an icon.

- **Inline Equation box.** A borderless box that enables you to add equations within text.

To add the graphics box, follow these steps:

1. Position the cursor where you want the box to be added.

2. Open the Graphics menu.

3. Choose Graphics Boxes. A small pop-up box appears, as shown in figure 16.3.

4. Choose the Create option. Now—take a deep breath—the rather frightening Create Graphics Box appears, as shown in figure 16.4.

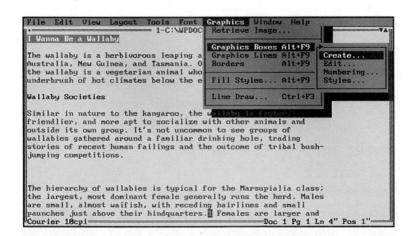

Figure 16.3
Graphics box options.

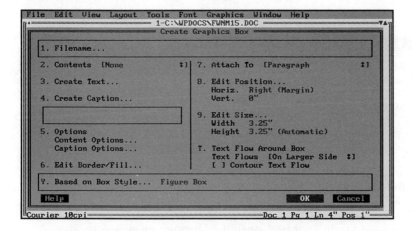

Figure 16.4
The Create Graphics Box has more options than you really want to deal with.

5. Here's what you do with the options:

Filename. Specify the graphics file you want to use.

Contents. Choose what will be displayed in the box.

Create Text. Create text for the image.

Create Caption. Add a caption to the image.

Options. Choose placement options for box contents and caption.

Edit Border/Fill. Control other art elements.

Attach To. Lets you attach the art to surrounding document items.

Edit Position. Specify the position of the art.

Edit Size. Enter the size of the image.

Text Flows Around Box. Control the placement of text around the image.

Based on Box Style. Choose the type of graphics box you want to create.

6. After entering all the options, click OK or press Enter.

WordPerfect then moves your text along the left side of the screen and places the graphics box on the right.

What I *Meant* To Do...

Don't like it? Too big? In the wrong place?

Don't sweat it.

You can edit the graphics you add to your WordPerfect document—if you don't expect too much of the word editing. Editing in this sense is not changing the look of the image, moving this person over here and this person over there. Editing when it comes to graphics means deleting, resizing, or rotating the graphic or changing the caption.

When you want to edit an image, open the Graphics menu and choose Graphics Box. Then choose Edit. The Select Box To Edit dialog appears, in which you need to specify the number of the box you want to change. Then click Edit Box.

Oh no. Not the Edit Graphics Box screen. This is the same dialog box as the Create Graphics Box, with a few modified options. Look through them—you'll recognize a few (see fig. 16.5).

Here, instead of Create Text, we've got Image Editor as option number 3. Also Create Caption has mysteriously changed to Edit Caption (go figure).

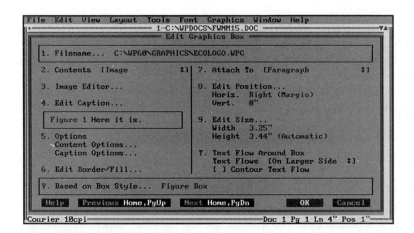

Figure 16.5
Image is everything.

Image Makeovers

In the Image Editor, you can resize, flip, rotate, and change the color of the image. First, select 3, Image Editor. The screen in figure 16.6 appears.

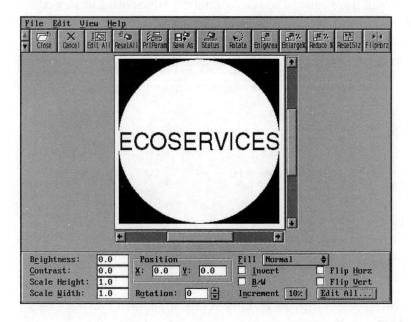

Figure 16.6
The mighty Image Editor.

Using the commands in the Edit menu and the Button Bar items, you can work with the image in the center of the screen. When you've got it where—and how—you want it, click Close in the Button Bar to return to the Edit Graphics Box screen.

What's Your Position?

> Crackle..crackle...Roger, Red Niner, this is Big Zero. Uh..what is our position, over?

You can use the Edit Position option in the Edit Graphics Box to move the image to a different position on the page. Remember when you pressed Enter, and WordPerfect just plopped the picture into the right side of the screen? Now you have a chance to put it where you want it.

Select option 8, Edit Position. The Paragraph Box Position dialog box appears (see fig. 16.7). The Paragraph Box Position says *Paragraph* because what you're changing is really the paragraph to which the graphics box is attached. With these options, you can control the Horizontal and Vertical position of the box.

Figure 16.7
Moving the box around.

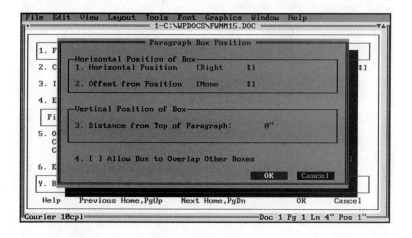

You can change the Horizontal Position to Left, Right (that's what it was), Full, or Centered. You can also choose the offset, the distance from the top of the paragraph, and whether you want the graphics box to overlap other boxes. When you're finished making changes (we chose Centered and Overlap), click OK or press Enter. There's that Edit Graphics Box screen again.

Rerunning Text

Remember how funky the text looked, all squished over to the left while the graphics box sat fat and happy on the right? Don't mind me: I'm just GFNAR (pronounced *guf-nar*) Griping For No Apparent Reason. You can change the way the text runs around the graphics box by using the Text Flow Around Box option.

Type T. The Text Flows option highlights. Click on the arrow to display your choices and select the one you want (we chose On Both Sides).

If you want WordPerfect to run the text up to the edge of the graphic instead of stopping at the edge of the box, click Contour Text Flow.

Click OK to complete the changes. You're returned to the document, and everything looks different. If you want to see the graphic, change to the Graphics Mode (see fig. 16.8).

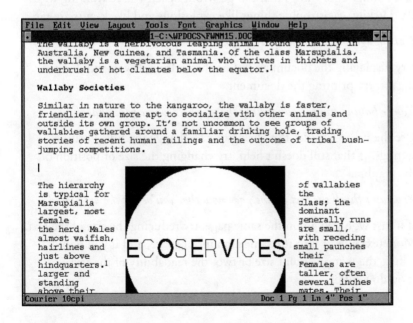

Figure 16.8
Changing the text flow.

They're Out To Get Us

There are a number of things that can go wrong when you're working with graphics. Luckily, catastrophic things like explosions and black-outs are rare.

Not enough memory to display graphics.

Try displaying the document in Graphics Mode. If you still don't see the art, try printing the document.

You're having trouble positioning the graphics where you want them.

Use the Edit Graphics Box dialog box to change the Edit Position settings. If that still doesn't help, try changing the size or position of the graphic.

You can't fit all the text on the page now that you've got the art placed.

If it just won't all go on the same page, try reducing the size of the text. More text will fit into the same amount of space, and if you only reduce the text one point size or two, the readability of the text shouldn't suffer.

You just can't leave the art alone.

This is known as Chronic Graphics Adjustment Syndrome, a problem that occurs when you just can't leave sleeping dogs lie and insist on fixing things that aren't broken. Have your officemate watch for that far-away, glazed look and repeat to yourself "I can overcome. I can overcome."

You're seeing graphics boxes before your eyes.

A new disorder, known as *box-sighted-ness*, that is prevalent among WordPerfect users. Blink several times in quick succession. If that doesn't help, you can send away for special 3-D glasses that can keep the condition from worsening.

Demon-Strations

Quick Clips

1. Position the cursor where you want the art to appear.

2. Open the Graphics menu.

3. Choose Retrieve Image.

4. Press F5 to display the GRAPHICS directory path and press Enter.

5. Choose the file you want from the File List; click Close.

Shadow Boxing

1. Put the cursor where you want the art.

2. Open the Graphics menu.

3. Choose Graphics Boxes.

4. Select Create.

5. When the Create Graphics Box dialog box appears, select the graphics file you want (in Filename); choose the Box style and any other necessary options.

6. Click OK or press Enter.

Summary

This encounter shed some light on one of those horrid things most new WordPerfect users have nightmares about: graphics. You can add to your document's eye-appeal dramatically by putting in your own art, whether that art is just a company logo, a drawn image, or clip art. And it's not as hard as it looks. The next encounter finishes off the book by explaining . . . (gulp) . . . merging documents.

Exorcises

1. True or false: You have to get clip art files before you can use WordPerfect's graphics features.

2. Name the two methods of adding art.

3. Put the following steps in order:

   _____ Select Create

   _____ Put the cursor where you want the art

   _____ Choose the art file you want to add

   _____ Add a caption, if necessary

   _____ Call your mother

   _____ Open the Graphics menu

   _____ Choose the box style

_____ Choose the Graphics Box command

_____ Click OK or press Enter

_____ Select Position and Size

4. True or false: After you position the art in the box, you cannot edit it.

5. Two options in the Edit Graphics Box dialog box control the way text runs around the art. What are they?

All Files Merge Right

Goal

To provide you with some emergency information just in case you are ever faced with—horror of horrors!—mail merging.

What You Will Need

Nerves of steel, a hard hat, and a sack lunch.

Terms of Enfearment

mail merging	merge printing
form	data
field	record

Briefing

The concept of *mail-merging*, also called *merge printing* by those not in-the-know, may be entirely new to you. If so, you may be, understandably, quaking (or quacking) in your boots by the end of this encounter.

Merging two documents is just what it sounds like: the process of taking this document and mixing it—like shuffling a deck of cards—into that document. The information in document 2 is used to plug holes in document 1.

Why would you be interested in such a thing? Well, remember those awful letters you get every month that sound like this:

Congratulations [Mr./Mrs./Ms.] *Your last name,*

You have been entered in our drawing and are guaranteed one of the following prizes:

- An outdated Sony walkman
- A 27-inch Toshiba color television
- A mink coat (with the mink still in it)

All you have to do, [*Your first name*], is call our 1-900 number between the hours of 8 and 5 to collect your prize.

Even those obnoxious letters had to be written somewhere. And the idea—being able to send out a form letter with the right names and information printed within the body of the letter—can be quite a boon for businesses.

Another common use of the mail-merge feature is producing mailing labels. That's something that makes even a die-hard WP enthusiast cringe. Oh, sure, it's easy to set up. But once you do, when you start to print, will your printer cooperate?

A Whole Lot of Merging Going On

Mail merging is really a simple concept. You create a letter with fill-in-the-blank spaces where the names should be. Then you create another file to store only the names. Then, through the miracle of mail merging, WordPerfect takes the names and plugs them in the blanks of the letter.

A lot better than creating one hundred copies of the same letter and entering the right names in each one, right?

Each of these fill-in-the-blank spaces is called a field. You can create fields to store different kinds of information, not just names. For example, you might include the following fields in a form letter about a new product your company is introducing:

> Firstname
> Lastname
> Title
> Company
> Address
> City
> State
> ZIP

Seems like a lot of information, but take a look at the letter shown in figure 17.1. In that letter, all these things are included as a matter of course. You probably type them so much you don't even notice.

If you wanted to send this letter to 100 clients, you would have your hands full erasing the names and addresses and typing in new ones 100 times. (Each letter, in mail-merge terms, is called a *record*.) Instead of all that hassle, WordPerfect gives you the option of making that letter a form into which all the information can be plugged automatically.

Ready to try it?

Figure 17.1
Frank's pushing his fuchsia fenders.

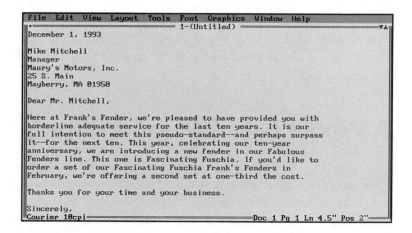

The Letter: Only a Shell

When you're ready to start your letter, open the Tools menu and select Merge. A small pop-up menu appears, as shown in figure 17.2.

Figure 17.2
Selecting the necessary options.

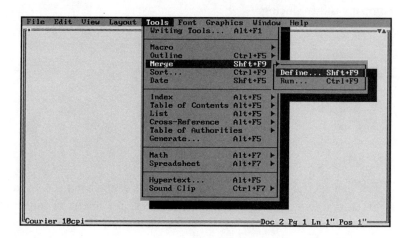

Choose the Define option. As you probably guessed, another screen appears. This one is the Merge Codes dialog box, and it gives you the choice of

selecting the form (or letter) or data (see fig. 17.3). For now, choose Form
by pressing Enter.

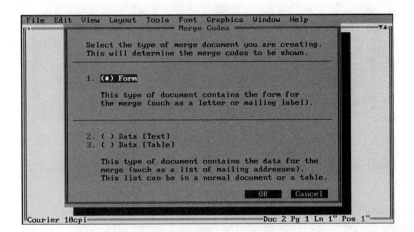

Figure 17.3
Opting for the form.

Oh, not another form...But there it is, the Merge Codes (Form File) dialog
box. This dialog box includes several options, but for our dip-a-toe-in-the-
water purposes here, we're just going to talk about fields (see fig. 17.4). Press
1 to select Field. The Parameter Entry box appears, as shown in figure 17.5.

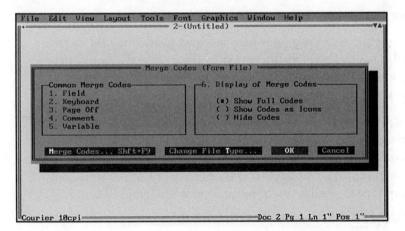

Figure 17.4
We're almost there.

Figure 17.5
Whew. Finally.

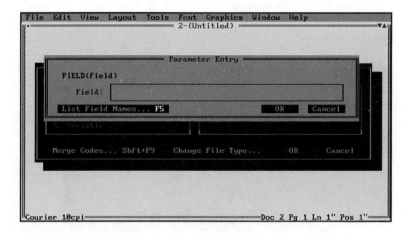

Type the name for the field you want. For example, *Firstname*. Then click OK or press Enter. You're thrown all the way back to the form, where the field is shown as

FIELD(Firstname)

But that's only one field. And you've got to enter a form full of them. You have to go through these steps every time?

There's a quicker way. (I know—*Now* you tell me!)

Position the cursor at the point where you want to add the field and press Shift+F9. That brings up the Merge Codes (Form File) dialog box right off the bat. Press 1 to select Field, and when the Parameter Entry (there's a friendly name) dialog box appears, type the name for the next field.

Continue entering fields in this way and then create the beef of your letter. If you want to include one of the fields in the body of the text, you don't have to go through the Shift+F9 thing again: this time, just highlight the field you want to use, copy it, and paste it into the document like you would any other text. Our finished letter (or form) is shown in figure 17.6.

When you're finished with the form, save the file.

> If you want to create mailing labels instead of a data form, just enter the fields as you want them to appear on the label.

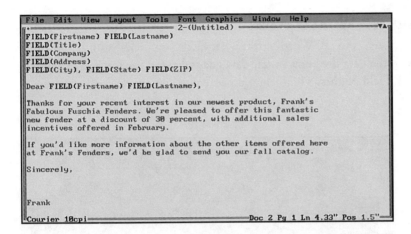

Figure 17.6
Just what the mailcarriers want—more form letters to deliver.

The Data, Looking for a Home

Now for the other hard part. We're going to make the data file. Start with a blank document. Then, open the Tools menu, choose Merge (remember that?), and when the little pop-up appears, choose Define again. The big Merge Codes box reappears, but this time, instead of selecting the form, you're going to choose Data.

There are two Data choices. One for text and one for table. This gives you two basic methods of entering the information. For our purposes, choose Text. The Merge Codes (Text Data File) dialog box appears (here we go again...) as shown in figure 17.7.

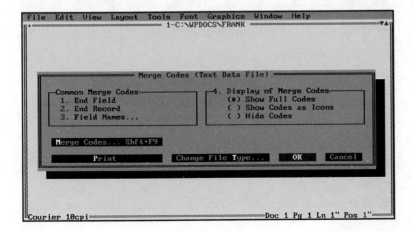

Figure 17.7
Starting the data file.

Telling WP What's What

Your next step is to tell WordPerfect what fields you included in the form. This way, the data file knows what data goes where in the form letter. Select option 3, Field Names. The Field Names dialog box appears, as shown in fig. 17.8.

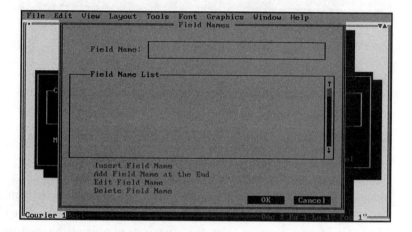

Type in each field name and press Enter after each one. When you're finished and all the names are listed, click OK or press Enter. WordPerfect inserts as the first entry in your data file an identifier line telling WordPerfect what fields to expect (see fig. 17.9).

Figure 17.9
The field's names, set and ready to go.

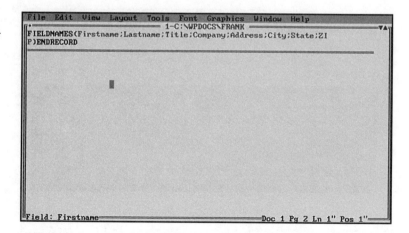

Pump in That Data

Now you're ready to put in the beef. Type the information for the first field.

This is important: You must enter the information in the same order the fields appear on the form. That means that if Firstname is first, type the first name of the person. Whatever data you enter in that first position will be plugged into the Firstname field, so if it's out of order, it's not going to make any sense.

After you've typed the data (in this case, Ralph), press Shift+F9 to display the Merge Codes box. Press 1 for End Field. WordPerfect inserts the code

ENDFIELD

and moves the cursor to the next line.

> If you have more than one field on the same line, use the backspace key to move the cursor back up to the line. The fields must be placed in the data file in the exact order they are positioned on the form in order for WordPerfect to match up the data and the letter.

After the last field on the form, press Shift+F9 and select 2, End Record. WordPerfect adds an ENDRECORD code and puts in a page break. Figure 17.10 shows a couple of entered records.

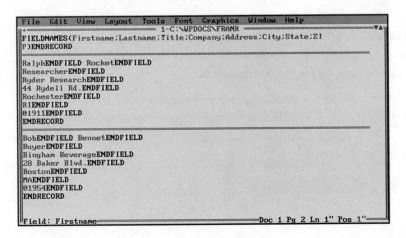

Figure 17.10
The data file with stuff entered.

Now save the file the normal way. (Remember the name, though.)

Mail-Merge Matchmaking

Okay, let's sit back and survey our work.

What do we have? One form, saved in a document file. One data file, saved as a document.

What do you think we do with them?

Ready, set, shuffle!

The actual process of merging the form file and data file is a simple one. Open the Tools menu, choose Merge, and select Run. The Run Merge dialog box appears (see fig. 17.11).

Figure 17.11
Preparing to merge.

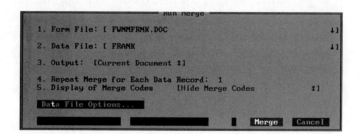

In the Form File box, enter the name of the form document (if you're unsure of the name, click the down-arrow to display the most recently used files). In the Data File box, enter the name of the data file. For Output, you can send the output to the printer, a file, another document, or a new (or current) document. Leave the setting as it is.

Click Merge and buckle in. Like lightning, WordPerfect merges those puppies and presents you with the offspring on-screen (see fig. 17.12).

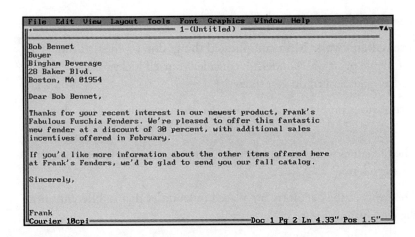

Figure 17.12
Ah, sweet success, at last I've found you.

Now go ahead and save your file. Then walk around the office primping and patting yourself on the back (those two things are hard to do at the same time). You deserve the recognition: you faced a worthy foe and lived to tell about it.

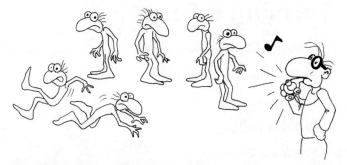

They're Out To Get Us

What's that? It *didn't* work? Oh, come on. Did you follow our flawless direction? Did your eye wander from the page—if only for an instant?

Oh, we're just kidding you.

Of course it didn't work. Most complicated things don't—the first time. (If your first merge print was wonderful, consider yourself lucky: The WordPerfect gods smiled on you today.)

The most obvious problem in a mail merge occurs when one of two things happen:

■ The filenames you enter on the data form are different from those on the form letter.

■ The fields in the data form are placed in an order that is different form the data form.

Keep trying; you'll get it. There are only so many things that can go wrong.

Demon-Strations

Forming a Form

1. Start with a new document.

2. Open the Tools menu.

3. Choose Merge.

4. Select Define.

5. Choose Form.

6. Press 1 (Field).

7. Click OK or press Enter.

8. Type the name of the field in the Field: box; click OK.

9. From the form, add other fields by pressing Shift+F9, pressing 1, entering the name of the field, and pressing Enter.

10. Save the file.

Doing Data

1. Start with another blank document.

2. Open the Tools menu and select Define.

3. Choose Data (Text).

4. Select option 3, Field Names.

5. Type the field names for the data file (the same ones you used in the form); press Enter after each name; click OK when you're through.

6. Type the data for the first field.

7. Press Shift+F9.

8. Press 1.

9. Continue entering data for each field, in the order the fields are used on the form. Press Shift+F9 and 1 after each entry.

10. After completing the entries for that form, press Shift+F9 and then 2 to enter the ENDRECORD code.

11. Remember to save the file when you're finished entering data.

Summary

This encounter brings you right up close to the biggest of all WordPerfect evils—mail merging—and then whisks you away again (kind of like a ride at DisneyWorld). With the completion of this encounter, you've mastered all basic WordPerfect fears and should be starting to emerge as a WordPerfect-confident (or at least non-bumbling) user.

This encounter also brings your initial experience with *Fear WordPerfect No More* to a close. Those little beasties weren't so bad, after all, were they?

But—

[queue ominous music]

what will happen when—gasp—they introduce WordPerfect 7.0?

Dunh-duh-*DAAHHHHH*!

Exorcises

1. True or false: Mail merging is something you use only to produce mailing labels.

2. What is a field?

3. Match the following:

   _____ Where you enter fields   a. The data file

   _____ Where you enter data   b. The data form

4. How many ways can you output the merged file?

5. Don't you think that mail merging is the coolest thing ever?

Exorcise Answers

You're not cheating, are you? Oh, come on—you really couldn't come up with those answers by looking them up in the chapter?

Well, shame on you. You realize you're wracking up bad karma, right?

1st Encounter

1. 6.0 (You're looking this up?)

2. Menus (or Tupperware—whichever's handiest)

3. False

4. c

5. For letters, for memos, and for reports. (Also, newsletters, books, brochures, or anything with words that you print.)

2nd Encounter

1. False

2. A cold boot freezes your foot, and a warm boot doesn't. Actually, a cold boot is when you turn on your machine after it has been sitting idle for a while. A warm boot is restarting the machine while power is already on.

3. The DOS prompt and the DOS Shell. The Shell has pull-down menus, and the prompt is just a prompt.

4. By using the mouse (point at the menu and click) or by using the keyboard (press the Alt key and the highlighted letter in the menu name).

5. "I Left My Heart in San Francisco."

3rd Encounter

1. Dairy, meat—oh, wait. QWERTY, cursor keys, numeric keypad, and special keys.

2. Move the cursor.

3. c

4. "Do it!" or "Go!" or "Get up off the couch, you!"

5. Point, click, double-click, and drag.

4th Encounter

1. _B_ Words

   _C_ Pages

   _A_ Lines

   _A_ Paragraphs

   _B_ Characters

   _C_ Screenfuls

2. Bars you can display along the bottom edge and right edge of the screen to help you scroll through a longer document using the mouse.

3. True

4. c

5. a (but I wish it was d)

5th Encounter

1. c

2. Times Roman and Courier.

3. Typeface, size, and style.

4. Bold, italic, underline, and normal.

5. Highlight it.

6th Encounter

1. Left, Right, Center, and Decimal.

2. To line things up.

3. Brussels sprout.

4. b

5. That's a big negatory, good buddy.

7th Encounter

1. Monospaced characters all take up the same amount of space, and proportional characters are assigned the amount of space necessary for the letter.

2. b

3. If you answered this question, you're more industrious than I am. But, for you overachievers: 7, 1, 3, 10, 2, 4, 8, 9, 6, 5.

4. b

8th Encounter

1. Save and Save As. Save As lets you save the file under a different name.

2. A kind of save that does it quick, without formatting codes.

3. Dream on. False.

4. Open is for files you've saved; Retrieve is for files you're pulling into other files.

5. True, but only after you press Home first.

9th Encounter

1. b

2. Use the mouse to highlight it, use Select, or write its phone number on the bathroom wall.

3. False

4. Select it, open the Edit menu, and choose Copy.

5. How true.

10th Encounter

1. Search just searches, and search and replace puts something else in place of the something found.

2. a

3. True; *someone* probably knows why.

4. Everything except c.

5. Oh come on. You're cheating on a Bonus Question?

11th Encounter

1. False

2. _b_ Speller Checker

   _a_ Thesaurus

   _c_ Grammatik

3. Press Alt+F1

4. True

5. b and f

12th Encounter

1. Four: Text, Graphics, Page, and Reveal Codes.

2. You can see graphics in Graphics view and headers and footers in Page view.

3. To see the secrets of your document and to delete codes that grew there accidentally.

4. b

5. I'm not sure, but it has something to do with Gerber oatmeal, broken hockey sticks, and missed piano lessons.

13th Encounter

1. _d_ Centered

   _c_ Full

   _a_ Left

   _b_ Right

2. Spreads out all lines, including headings

3. When you're using columns, or when you're feeling really defensive

4. Left, your left, your left...

5. e (and d, too)

14th Encounter

1. c

2. False

3. Paragraph Spacing and First Line Indent.

4. Position the cursor and press Ctrl+Enter.

5. Gosh, I hate these, don't you? The first is Position the cursor, and the last is click OK. Do what you want in the middle.

15th Encounter

1. A header is at the top; and a footer's at the bottom of the page.

2. A footer is something that prints on every page that has no ties in the text; a footnote is a note placed at the bottom of the page that clarifies a point in text.

3. Got me.

4. Send them to Kelly Dobbs, c/o Brady Books.

5. Company name, date, your name, and the document title.

16th Encounter

1. False. WordPerfect comes with graphics files.

2. You can add graphics free-form or bring it into a graphics box.

3. Why, oh *why*, did I write this question in the first place? The order is 3, 1, 6, 7, 10, 2, 5, 4, 9, 8.

4. False

5. Text Flow and Contour Text Flow.

17th Encounter

1. False

2. A place in Indiana where they grow lots of corn.

3. b and then a

4. To a new (or the current) document, to the printer, to a file, or to another document you specify.

5. No. Those little sports socks are the coolest thing ever.

Index

Fear No... More

A New Computer Book Series for the Absolute Beginner

Never before has mastering a computer been so practical, fun, simple, and completely panic-free. Filled with off-beat characters, practical "demon-strations," and skill-building "excorcises," FEAR...NO MORE focuses exclusively on the needs of the first-time computer user.

Now Available

FEAR MACS NO MORE
ISBN 1-56686-082-2
$15.95

- Developed by award-winning author Danny Goodman!

- Illustrated in 2-color!

FEAR EXCEL NO MORE
Version 4.0 for the Mac
ISBN 1-56686-083-0
$15.95

FEAR WINDOWS
NO MORE
ISBN 1-56686-081-4
$15.95

- Makes learning the computer fun and challenging!

- Available for Mac & Windows

FEAR EXCEL
NO MORE
Version 4.0 for Windows
ISBN 1-56686-084-9
$15.95

ISBN	Qty	Title	Price
1-56686-082-2		Fear Macs No More	$15.95
1-56686-081-4		Fear Windows No More	$15.95
1-56686-083-0		Fear Excel No More for the Mac	$15.95
1-56686-084-9		Fear Excel No More for Windows	$15.95

Send to: **Brady/Fear Titles**
Prentice Hall Computer Publishing
11711 N. College Ave., Suite 140
Carmel, IN 46032
or toll free: 1-800-428-5331

Subtotal _____
State sales tax _____
Shipping & Handling ($2.50/title) _____
TOTAL _____

☐ Check ☐ VISA ☐ MasterCard ☐ American Express

Acct. # _____ Signature _____

Ship to: Name _____ Company _____

Address _____

City _____ State _____ Zip _____